Developments of Democracy in Yemen

Amat Al-Alim As-Suswa (ed.)

Professors World Peace Academy - Middle East

Coyright © 1994 by the Professors World Peace Academy

Professors World Peace Academy
2710 West University Ave., Suite 47
St. Paul, MN 55114-1016, U.S.A.

Amat Al-Alim As-Suswa, editor

ISBN 3-87997-228-1

Layout and Reproduction: Fritz Piepenburg
Cover Design: Adnan Gumman
Colour Separation: Graphic Art Center, Sanaa
Printing: Horizons for Printing and Publishing, Sanaa

 Klaus Schwarz Verlag, Berlin

Contents

Amat al-Alim as-Suswa
Introduction 7

Muhammad Shahir Hasan
The Development of Democracy in the Example of the People's General Congress 14
    The National Movement and the Struggle for Liberty
    and Democracy 14
    The Road of Democracy in the Example
    of the People's General Congress 17
    The Political Activities of the People's General Congress 20
    The Formation of Unions and Popular Societies 21

Dr. Ahmad Muhammad al-Kibsi
From the Holy Charter to the Permanent Constitution and the National Charter 27
    Evaluating the Imamate from the Viewpoint
    of Political Participation 28
    The Nationalist Movement and Its Demands 29
    The Development of the New Political System 31
    Genesis of the 1970 Permanent Constitution 34
    The Genesis of the National Charter 36
    Characteristics of the Permanent Constitution
    and the National Charter 39
    Statement of Public Freedoms and Rights
    in the Permanent Constitution and the National Charter 42
    Councils and Assemblies 47
    The Shura Council of 1971 48
    The People's Constituent Assembly 48
    The Shura Council of 1988 49

Ahmad Muhammad al-Harbi
The Cooperative Movement: a Basis for Democratic Development 59
- Cooperative Work in Yemen's History 59
- Yemeni Cooperative Work - Genesis and Early Achievements 61
- Cooperatives as Forms of Social Solidarity 63
- Forms of Cooperation and the Employment of Democratic Means 65
- The 26 September Revolution of 1962 and the New Structure of Cooperatives 66
- Cooperative Democracy in Practice 68
- Local Development Associations and the Development of Cooperative Democracy 71
- Democracy in the Daily Operations of the Cooperatives 73
- Historic Significance of Democracy within the Cooperative Movement and its Development within the Framework of the Local Councils for Cooperative Development 75

Dr. Sa'd Eddin Ibrahim
Winds of Democracy Blowing over Arab Soil 79
- Between Autumn in Cyprus and Spring in Amman 79
- Winds of Democracy in Arabia 81
- The Problem of Despotism and Problems of Democracy 82

Dr. Ahmad Abdurahman Sharafuddin
The Basic Principles of Election Laws 88
- The Principle of Universal Suffrage 89
- The Principle of Free Elections 90
- The Principle of Personal Representation 90
- The Principle of Equal Participation 91

Ilham Muhammad Mane'
Algeria's Election Experiment 93
Concepts of Democracy 94
From a One-Party to a Multi-Party System 94
The National Liberation Front 95
The Islamic Salvation Front 96
The Front of Socialist Powers 97
The Pro-Democracy Movement 97
Political Reforms 97
Process and Results of the 1991 Parliamentary Elections .. 101
A Possible Interpretation of the Events 103

Muhammad Ja'far Qasim
A Critical View of the Draft Law for Elections 107
The Period Preceding the Establishment of the two Yemeni Republics 107
The Election Laws of the two Republics of Yemen (1962 - 1990) 109
The Election Law of 1992 111
The Principles of Competitive Elections 112
Organization of Election Campaigns by the Candidates 112
Equality in Campaigning 113
Organization of the Voters 114
Division of the Electorates 115
Organization of the Balloting 115
The Electoral System within the Draft Law 116
Neutrality of the Government and its Organizations during the Election Process 117
Decisions on Electoral Disputes (Appeals) 118

Ahmad Ali al-Wada'i
Contemplations on Unification and Democracy in Yemen 122
Questions to Our Newborn Democracy 122
Marriage between Unification and Democracy 123

Dr. Mansur Aziz az-Zindani
Third-World Democracies and the New World Order 127
Challenges to our Young Democracy 128
Defending our Democracy from the Big Friends 128

Dr. Muhammad Ahmad as-Sa'idi
Safeguarding the Future of Democracy in Yemen 131
Understanding democracy 132
No Democracy without Political Freedom 133
The Right Time for Democracy in Yemen 135
Guarantees for Democracy in Yemen 136

Fritz Piepenburg
The 1993 Parliamentary Elections in Yemen 140
Setting the Stage 141
The Political Landscape after Unification 142
The Supreme Election Committee 147
Choosing the Constituencies 149
The Registration of Voters 151
Registration of Candidates 154
The Day of Balloting 156
Results 158
Accusations of Fraud and Deception 162

Amat al-Alim as-Suswa
Women and Democracy in Yemen 167
Two Roads to Women's Emancipation in Yemen 167
The Position of the Yemeni Women in Today's Society 169
Women and the Parliamentary Elections of 1993 171
Women's Issues in the Party Programs 173
The Yemeni Women's Union 175
Conclusions 176

Introduction

The seminar papers compiled in this book present a good overview of the development of democracy and its practical application in Yemen. They also shed light on the unique features of this particular democratic experience and will help in deciding on how to create political awareness among our people.

The paper written by **Muhammad Shahir Hasan** explains the beginning of Yemen's democratic course with the establishment of the People's General Congress. This major party became one of many political organizations that encouraged and participated in the introduction of a multi-party system, culminating in the parliamentary elections of April 27, 1993. The author comes up with interesting details and facts about this early period of Yemeni democracy.

The original meaning of democracy, in the words of de Tocqueville, is "the system of self-rule", which simply means that cooperatives, schools, scientific institutes and other civil institutions can take care of themselves without government interference. The cooperatives, in particular, seem to hold the potential of becoming an effective organizational base for our society, especially after the abolition of the one-party system. Once organized properly, they will become the training ground for applying and practicing democracy.

The same holds true for unions and other social institutions, which are independent from the state or certain party organizations. They form the fertile ground for democratic interactions among the members of society, thus guaranteeing the continuation and growth of democracy itself.

The paper presented by **Dr. Ahmad Muhammad al-Kibsi** was selected because it gives an overview of our understanding of democracy since the Movement of the Free Yemenis in 1948 and the drafting of the Holy National Charter up to the present days. The paper focuses on developments taking place in the former North Yemen before unification. A university professor and specialist in the field of political science, Dr. al-Kibsi traces the very early roots of democratic development in Yemen. He also explains the constitutional and legal foundations for our current democratic system, much of which is based on a national dialogue that resulted in the compilation of the National Charter under the umbrella of the People's General Congress.

Ahmad Muhammad al-Harbi provides a historical overview of the forms and developments of cooperatives prevalent in the Yemeni villages. For ages these villages have known the meaning of social solidarity in the form of cooperation, especially in the area of agriculture and irrigation. Al-Harbi not only explains the various forms of cooperation, but also the internal power structure of the Yemeni villages and their indigenous ways of solving problems.

These forms of cooperation and methods of solving disputes have their roots in the pre-Islamic age and evolved over a period of thousands of years. It is impossible to pinpoint the exact beginning of these structures, which seem to have always been a part of our rural and urban societies.

During the last few years, the Yemeni cooperatives have been experiencing a tremendous leap of progress. They are responsible for supplying the rural population, which still constitutes some 88% of our entire population, with much needed services.

In fact, the very rise of the cooperative movement bears witness to the inability of the central government to provide all social services required by the population. The destiny of these cooperatives will be their evolution into decentralized structures of local government and administration. This, incidentally, is one of the goals of all our parties, big or small.

Ahmad al-Harbi is himself an active member of the cooperative movement. His paper, therefore, not only deals with the historic development of the cooperatives, but provides a wealth of personal experience as well. It is not difficult to imagine that these cooperatives will quickly pick up the concept of democratic participation as it was already envisioned by the National Charter and confirmed by the public referendum of 1981.

Dr. Sa'd Eddin Ibrahim describes in his paper how the "winds of democracy" are blowing over the countries of the Third World, including the Arab World. Concerning the Arab World in general and the Arabian Peninsula in particular, Yemen seems to play a pioneering role in the development of democracy. This is of considerable importance to other parts of the world since the peninsula holds the planet's greatest resources in oil and gas. Also its economy is closely intertwined with that of Europe and America.

The following three papers were presented during a seminar on election systems and the future of democracy in Yemen. **Dr. Ahmad Abdurahman Sharaf Eddin**, a specialist in law, explains the basic principles of democracy and their effect upon the peaceful and stable development of society. Dr. Sharaf Eddin mentions the need to extend the right to vote to the community of Yemeni emigrants and those traveling within Yemen as long as they fulfill the two basic requirements of Yemeni nationality and age. He explains the basic principles of the Election Law, such as equality and the requirement of voting in person, i.e., not by delegation. This requirement of voting personally was blatantly disregarded in the recent elections in Algeria, where husbands were allowed to vote in place of their wives, even without written consent.

Ms. Ilham Muhammad Mane' gives a careful analysis of the background and circumstances surrounding the problematic development in Algeria. She explains the Algerian election experiment, which, although it held the promise of finally ending the long-standing one-party rule by establishing a new democratic multi-party system, resulted in something entirely different.

Even though the paper written by Mane' specifically deals with the Algerian election experience, it is certainly a very relevant case for other parts of the Arab world. It gives a vivid example of the highly destructive consequences that ensue if just one of the basic principles of democracy is altered. In fact, these consequences threaten the very stability of the country and undermine all possibilities for a future peaceful transfer of power in the future.

Dr. Muhammad Ja'far Qasim comes up with some critical remarks about the current Yemeni Election Law. He does so to make sure that the democratic experiment in Yemen can start from a sound basis. Dr. Qasim draws upon a wealth of information and knowledge of different election laws, especially from European countries, yet does not neglect Arab, African, or Asian nations. There is much that Yemen can learn from the experiences of the countries that preceded it in the establishment of parliamentary democracy. The paper discusses in detail the legal conditions needed to give the election process proper direction. It also sheds light on the weak points and pitfalls of our existing Election Law.

A number of pointed questions are asked in the paper presented by **Ahmad Ali al-Wadi'i**. According to his view, democracy in Yemen took on a liberal Western pattern and became necessary because of national re-unification. Thus, he views democracy in Yemen from a new and unique perspective. The author expresses his worries about the continuation and growth of democracy in Yemen, which is built on weak foundations. People are much more conscious of unification than of democracy. He even envisions a scenario wherein Yemen remains united, but abandons the democratic system. This, of course, depends on the success or failure of the political forces responsible for the protection of democracy. More social studies will have to be conducted to identify these forces and possible ways of strengthening them. Could these forces be strong enough to turn the initial momentum of our nation's sudden and rather unexpected surge of democracy into a stable and continuous development? Is there a possibility that the Yemeni people would let go of democracy? Are not the two leading parties of the former South and North Yemen the chief advocates for the adoption of a modern democratic system? It seems that these questions have much to do with the economy. Economic success contributes a great deal to the stability of democracy, whereas economic failure leads to its disintegration.

Dr. Mansur Aziz az-Zindani is concerned in his paper with the influence of the main powers (the developed countries) upon the young democracies of the Third World. The countries of the southern hemisphere are quite happy with their newly acquired democracies. They view democracy as a means to solve all political corruption and other long-standing problems and issues. However, these hopes are surrounded internally and externally by threats and dangers. Dr. az-Zindani enumerates some of the external threats that come with the embrace of a certain type of democracy. He urges developing countries to reject the mere adoption of the pattern of Western democracy, whereby a whole new value system is being adopted as well. He contends that this new value system will eventually erode the original traditions and characteristics of the Third World country.

Dr. Muhammad Ahmad as-Saidi explains what he feels are the prerequisites for democratic development in Yemen. Among those, he lists economic and political stability, a broader participation of the public in the decision making process and unrestricted freedom of expression. Dr. as-Saidi defends the hypothesis which states that the seeds of democracy are already present in the tribal systems of Third World countries, especially in African countries that have experienced colonialism. He rejects the idea that democracy is a phenomenon implanted by Western countries into their former colonies. In his paper, he lists further conditions, such as a sound constitutional and legal system and an increasing involvement by independent social organizations and institutions in politics. Supporting the process of decentralization and giving new political power to the local governments is another important prerequisite for the smooth unfolding of democratic development.

The paper presented by **Fritz Piepenburg** gives a brief overview of the beginnings of democracy in former North and South Yemen. He seems to imply that early developments in the South were influenced by Western ideas, as a result of the colonial establishment. The examples of democratic developments in the southern regions of Lahij, Abyan and Aden are cited from a book written by Dr. Qaid Tarabush. In his introduction Mr. Piepenburg also describes the practice of shura (consultation) in Islam as a kind of "religious democracy". Without clarifying his own viewpoint on this issue, he mentions that some people put this practice on an equal level with modern democracy. Later on he seems to support this opinion by stating that parliamentary democracy is by no means the only form of democracy, even though it might be the most advanced.

His presentation of what happened on April 27, 1993, aided by tables, graphs and maps, and based on official documents of the Supreme Election Committee, gives a complete picture of the first parliamentary elections in re-united Yemen.

The paper by **Amat al-Alim as-Suswa** deals with the issue of women and democracy. It attempts to shed light on yet another aspect of Yemeni life. The paper points to the vast cleft that often exists between purely theoretical concepts and the cultural and political realities regulating our daily lives. For example, during the 1993 elections, the gap between what was presented in the election programs of various parties and the reality of political practice, especially concerning women candidates, turned out to be immense.

Introduction

Recent events, especially the 70-day-war against the separatists (May 5th till July 7th 1994), will not alter the road of democracy chosen by the Republic of Yemen. This was confirmed by a proclamation on part of the Presidential Council in July 1994. In this proclamation, the adherence by the leadership to democratic values and principles, such as freedom of expression and a multi-party political system, was confirmed. Thus the original political direction, upon which the unified state was based in 1990, will be preserved.

All of the papers collected in this book were among those presented in three different seminars. The first seminar was jointly organized by the People's General Congress and the Professors' World Peace Academy in Sana'a under the title "Democratic Developments in Yemen and the Arab World" on June 22-23, 1989. The second was entitled "Electoral Systems and the Future of Democracy in Yemen" and was organized by the People's General Congress/Sana'a University Branch on February 16-17, 1992. The third was sponsored by the People's General Congress/District II of the capital on May 17-18, 1992, and dealt with "Prerequisites for the Future of Democracy in Yemen".

We hope that the selection of presentations and research papers included in this book will help the reader gain a deeper understanding of what is happening with our newly born democracy in Yemen. It is a democracy heavily influenced by our special circumstances, such as the deep cultural roots of our society and its complicated structure. Because of our heritage of a complicated social fabric, we may well be one of the most conservative societies in the Arab world, socially, ideologically and politically.

Finally, we should not forget to express our gratitude to the People's General Congress, which, by organizing the aforementioned seminars, opened the door for the presentation of a great variety of thoughts and viewpoints on our newly born democracy by academics and party representatives. Our gratitude also goes to the Professors' World Academy, which co-sponsored the first seminar and financed the compilation and printing of this book. A final word of thanks goes to Dr. Muhammad Sharaf Eddin, who translated most of the papers into English.

Amat al-Alim as-Suswa
Sanaa, September 1994

PART I

Democratic Developments in Yemen and the Arab World

Selected papers of a two-day seminar jointly sponsored by the People's General Congress / Yemen and the Professors' World Peace Academy / Middle East, June 22-23, 1989 in Sanaa

The Development of Democracy in the Example of the People's General Congress

by Muhammad Shahir Hasan

The 26 September Revolution succeeded in changing life in Yemen decisively. It moved forward the wheel of history by giving the Yemeni people their just role in building their society according to the unique characteristics of the Yemeni nation. These changes were achieved by the 26 September Revolution through public struggle motivated by revolutionary and patriotic will. The many achievements and results that changed the lives of the people in our country cost the lives of countless martyrs. Before the outbreak of the Revolution, the people of our country were suffering from injustice, backwardness and corruption. Now, our daily life is smiling with freedom, generosity, democracy, and national self-determination. We achieved a lot in terms of development, modernization of government organizations, and the improvement of working conditions. The Revolution's main concern revolved around the modernization of society. The human being was considered the first goal of and the means for development at the same time. The Revolution was capable of giving a new form and shape to society, modernizing the life of each citizen by strengthening his faith in himself and his capabilities of building and developing his life according to his own free will. He has been actively participating in the revolutionary course, overcoming difficulties and challenges and transcending the dark ages of the past.

The National Movement and the Struggle for Liberty and Democracy

Yemen before the 26 September Revolution lived in an age of tyranny and did not know any type of democracy or organized public participation whatsoever. The Imam held all the powers in his hands and made each final decision, be it trifle or of national importance. A formal political organization was completely lacking, except in the fields of levying taxes and arresting opponents. There was no constitution which clarified power structures and responsibilities delegated to lower levels. There was hardly any formal announcement of law, much less a clarification of possible interpretation.

This terrible constitutional and organizational backwardness was a part of the overall backwardness. The lack of public participation led to the concentration of political power in the hands of one person. The first steps towards rectification failed, and the Imam did not heed the advice given to him and his government in order to satisfy the demands of the people. He was not willing to let the people go beyond their lives of deprivation, injustice and ignorance, thereby catching up with the developments of the 20th century. The movement of the Free Yemenis worked for this noble cause, facing the threats of the Imam. Many cultural and social organizations were founded by the people themselves as a first step towards opposing the tyranny. The Imam reacted by terrorizing those who opposed his tyrannical regime. The Free Yemenis, however, stayed determined in rejecting injustice, backwardness and ignorance, and were able to gather support from a growing number of people. They were joined by educated people, soldiers and tribesmen. All these efforts aimed at destroying the tyrannical one-man-rule and exchanging it for a constitutional one.

The will of our people proved to be victorious and the tyrant was overthrown by the Free Yemenis in 1948 who killed Imam Yahia and announced the Holy Charter and the establishment of a constitutional government and parliamentary system. The Revolution was aimed at bringing Yemen into the age of enlightenment. The Holy Charter verified the right of the people to build and actively participate in constitutional organizations which were specified in that Holy National Charter. This was in line with developments in other civilized nations and in complete agreement with the true teachings of Islam.

The Charter furthermore stated that political power should be delegated according to the will of the people, considering the people to be the legal authority to appoint their ruler or to remove him from his position. The Holy Charter specified that the ruler should be appointed by representatives of the people. The ruler's duty was to abide with the laws given by Allah, using his powers exclusively for the sake of the people. The Holy Charter also specified the scope of governmental powers. It specified the need for preparing elections for parliament as the law-giving institution. Steps were to be taken to ensure the participation of all Yemenis inside and outside the country. Furthermore, it urged a continuous struggle against ignorance, poverty and disease, overcoming the current backwardness inherited from the rule of the Hamid ad-Din family.

This constitutional revolution was a popular attempt to embark upon a new road in the life of the people. It verified the importance of democratic consultation, considering it one of the fundamentals in any political system. This is demanded by the Islamic religion and therefore considered to be a political and religious duty. Our people's quest for these basic rights will prevail, no matter how much tyrannical rulers or backward circumstances might want to undermine it.

And even though the failure of this revolution turned Yemen back into the darkness of a tyrannical government by a single person without any hope for public participation, it created a powerful tremor in the depth of the Yemeni people. Over a lapse of time, these events became the driving force for arousing the people's awareness of their national rights, pushing them on the road of revolutionary change. The sacrifices that followed the failure of the 1948 Revolution were substantial. However, it was an important basis for future developments.

The rule of Ahmad Hamid ad-Din was no less severe than that of his father. It also had the typical signs of backwardness and tyranny, injustice, bloodshedding and ignorance. Yemen under his reign again did not know any sort of public participation in government politics or legislation. There was no constitution, no public laws, and no room for political organizations. There was only the power of the Imam, while the people were suffering from hunger, ignorance, disease and injustice.

The uprisings of 1955 caused the Free Yemenis to reconsider their standpoint. They decided to go beyond the stage of constitutional monarchy and call for the establishment of a republican, Islamic, and democratic system.

The struggle of our people continued during the following years, such as exemplified in the assassination attempts by al-'Ulufi, al-Laqiyyah, al-Handawanah, various tribes and some units of the army. There were students' demonstrations and other uprisings which acted like a vanguard until the final outbreak of the 26 September Revolution in 1962, changing the Yemeni situation in all walks of public life. The goals of the Revolution represented the fundamental desires of our people, namely freedom and progress.

The circumstances influencing the course of the Revolution in its early phases were not favorable for building a truly democratic society, as specified in the 4th goal of the Revolution. However, the will for democracy was always there and has been expressed in many conferences and congresses.

In that spirit the Congress of Khamir was held between May 2nd and 5th, 1965. This meeting prompted the convention of further conferences, such as the General Congress of the People's Revolutionary Union, which took place in Sana'a between January 18th and 20th, 1967. It was followed by the Saba Congress on 3 March of the same year. The Congress of the Learned Men of Yemen took place in January 1968, followed by the Conference of Public Opposition in Sana'a on 4 March 1968, the Conference of the Military and Security Forces in Sana'a on 11 March 1969, the People's Congress in Sana'a on 14 March 1969, as well as other conferences and congresses. All of them studied the respective phase of development and issued recommendations for formulating the basic principles of public and parliamentary participation in the future government.

After having been victorious in destroying its enemies, the Revolution entered into the phase of setting the foundations for a modern central state. A clear sign of its success was the enactment of the permanent constitution and the establishment of the parliamentary council, which at that time was called the People's Constituent Assembly. It was a good training ground for practicing democracy. Another important sign of democratic development was the establishment of the Local Development Associations.

The Road of Democracy in the Example of the People's General Congress

The decision to draft a National Charter (NC) was a necessary step towards fulfilling national aspirations. It followed the logic of the Revolution, which demands constant evaluation of experiments and standpoints. The people's desires for development and progress could be fulfilled by overcoming the period of spiritual and political vacuum, which preceded the age of the NC and which became a serious threat to the revolutionary cause, the independence of our people and the aspirations for national unity. There was a lack of a clear theory for realizing the principles of the Revolution on a national level.

Therefore, the creation of the NC was absolutely necessary. It was to be based on the legislation of the shari'ah and would embody the goals of the Revolution, realizing the hopes of the people and protecting them from any possible form of disruption. It became an answer to the "serious and ardent search for elevating society to a higher revolutionary stage, from the level of democratic slogans to the level of democratic realization".

Studies were undertaken by national representatives of all the different social levels of our society in order to formulate the NC. A council was formed from among the members of the People's Constituent Assembly. Several representatives and leaders of society were chosen to also join this council. Next, branch committees were established, each concentrating on a special area. All these activities finally led to the formulation of the National Charter, which the President presented to the Advisory Council for further discussion. The matter did not stop there, but the President decided to present it to an expanded meeting consisting of the Advisory Council, the entire cabinet, the provincial governors, and other officials from military and civil organizations. All of them agreed that this project should be presented to the people.

Republican Decree No. 5 was announced in 1980, calling for the creation of a Council of National Dialogue, which was to be the first step in the establishment of the People's General Congress (PGC). Representatives of various parts of our society convened in order to formulate the NC. This council was working for approximately two years. The project finally was submitted to the people for appraisal and commentaries. A great number of people participated with a high level of awareness and responsibility. The plebiscite was conducted under the supervision of the Council for National Dialogue by distributing written manifests. These were then returned to the council after each citizen had freely expressed his views on each paragraph and each section of the draft. The council would then proceed to incorporate the public view by revising the wording of the NC.

Eventually, Republican Decree No. 19 was issued in 1981, limiting the members of the PGC to 1,000 representatives. 70% of these members were to be elected by the people in free elections and 30% would be appointed by the government. This congress was meant to review the NC in light of the written comments submitted by the people and to draft a final version and decide on ways for implementation.

The President issued a number of republican decrees, specifying the following points:
- Republican Decree No. 28 of 1981 aiming at the formation of a high council and branch councils for supervising the elections of the Local Development Associations in the third election period. These councils were also given responsibility to supervise the election of representatives into the PGC.
- Presidential Decree No. 53 of 1982 fixed the election date for electing the representatives for the PGC.
- Presidential Decree No. 54 of 1982 fixed the date for convening the PGC.

The first convention of the PGC took place between August 24th and 29th, 1982. Among its most important decisions were the acceptance of the NC in its final version and the decision to uphold the institution of the PGC as a framework for political activities of all parts of society.

Thus, all patriotic elements of society confirmed the peaceful principles of the Revolution as the basic road for realizing a better future.

They especially agreed on the following points:
- to employ means of dialogue for combating dangerous divisions and for jointly building the country;
- to allow the free expression of different viewpoints by acknowledging the possibility of different roads for achieving the same solution; differences should be resolved by peaceful means and objective dialogue, always keeping in mind the goal of national unity clearly formulated in the principles of the Revolution;

- dialogue in a free and democratic atmosphere will always be the way to cure friction;
- while acknowledging the importance of dialogue, there are yet certain principles and matters above discussion, such as our Islamic religion, the Revolution and its goals, and the independence of our country and its sovereignty;
- the results of the national dialogue represent a genuine and objective alternative to the perils of division and seclusion; national dialogue is the much better choice in realizing a better life for all people by confirming the principle of public political participation in the process of decision making.

Membership in the People's General Congress as a political body is subject to the following rules:

- It is decided by secret, free and direct vote; representatives come from the far ends of the country and people can chose those personalities who are famous for being public-minded and carrying public responsibilities.
- Representatives of the PGC have certain duties and are also granted certain rights; duties and rights are derived from the basic order and the goals specified in the NC agreed upon earlier by all parts of society.
- Members perform their activities and duties according to the program decided by the people and formulated in the NC, which is not a ready ideology or theory nor an expression of a certain political or social group; thus the activities of the PGC cannot be judged by just one group of people.
- Establishing the PGC made it possible to heal the political discrepancies and differences and to advance the search for the best method of solving problems since the outbreak of the September Revolution.
- Political activities took place within the framework of the specifications laid down by the Congress and its internal structure; it became a forum for democracy and the basis of the thought of the NC ; thus, after the establishment of the PGC there was no place left for the establishment of political parties.
- Throughout the past years, the PGC has achieved good results and acted successfully in bridging political differences and averting political fragmentation into a number of parties; the Congress took its place among other political organizations and parties of brotherly and friendly nations; there are flourishing relations with those foreign political organizations.

The Political Activities of the People's General Congress

Political work has been lifted to a higher level and people were brought to a deeper understanding of political activities on the basis of the NC. The branch committees also supervised the implementation of decisions and recommendations passed by PGC, by the Permanent Committee and by the branch congresses on the provincial levels. Social energies are being channeled into development programs drawn up for the people with a view to raise the level of education by combating illiteracy. The continuous work of these branch councils guarantees the implementation of the contents of the NC by its members first. Transferred to other people, a broader base of public participation is being realized. It was absolutely necessary to divide the branch congresses into small working groups on the level of the district, the village and the city quarter. Each member of the entire membership of the Congress can contribute his part and thus have a sense of importance about his membership.

Forums for political guidance were created as an important aspect of the activities of the PGC. They include the organization of studies and lectures. Other forums deal with various intellectual, political and economic issues and matters relating to our political experiment. They take place every Thursday and can be considered miniature congress meetings, addressing various issues and problems through lectures and studies prepared by a Standing Committee. They are considered a platform for constant contact between the leadership and the people. Through them it becomes possible to identify the worries and requirements of the citizens and to learn about their views on various matters of concern to our present and future. They also increase the level of political knowledge and awareness.

The establishment of the National Charter Institute constitutes an important stage in raising the level of political education. Graduates will play their part in spreading and consolidating the principles and concepts of the NC among the people.

Democratic elections for choosing representatives to the PGC took place in July 1985 in all parts of the republic. It was an extraordinary event, in which 18,000 members were elected; one representative for each 500 citizens. 70,000 candidates wanted to take on responsibility for politics and development. The expansion of the PGC membership was approved by the PGC in its second ordinary session held from August 21st to 23rd, 1984.

To fulfill the role and tasks of the PGC, its branches had to spread to all districts and villages, for the purpose of spreading its provisions, objectives, plans and programs to all citizens on Yemeni territory. The people who are the decision makers and the authors of the Charter must express their reactions continuously and add new blood to the ranks of political leadership in order to strengthen the implementation of the Charter and to realize further democratic gains and developments by fostering a growing political consciousness.

Expanding the membership of the PGC envisioned the following developments:
- increasing the organizational effectiveness of the PGC;
- halting attempts of penetration into the society by unwanted elements;
- providing for a broad popular participation in organized political work;
- expanding the base of popular participation in the government by allowing the people to participate in legitimate political actions through the PGC;
- attracting the largest possible number of active citizens in the countryside and the towns in order to benefit from their activities, thus achieving the objectives of the NC.

The Formation of Unions and Popular Societies

After the President's historic call upon the workers to form their own unions, the following labor unions were established:
- Union of Laborers of the Textile and Spinning Factory
- Union of the Bajil Cement Factory Workers
- Union of Transport, Forwarding and Clearing Workers of the Sana'a Governorate
- Union of the General Cotton Company
- Union of the Workers of the Amran Cement Factory
- Union of the Workers of the Electricity Corporation
- Union of Transport, Forwarding and Clearing Workers of the Taiz Governorate
- Union of Transportation Workers of the Sana'a Governorate
- Union of the Workers of the Water and Sewerage Authority
- Union of the Electricity Workers in Hodeidah
- Union of the Electricity Workers in Taiz
- Union of the Workers and Employees of Yemen Airways
- Union of the Drivers of the Sana'a-Taiz Route
- Union of the Drivers of the Amran Province.

Existing trade unions already established in February 1984 set up a preparatory committee for the formation of the General Confederation of Trade Unions of the Yemen Arab Republic. They applied to the Ministry of Social Affairs and Labor for approval to establish the confederation and to convene its first meeting. This was greatly encouraged by the President himself who called for the establishment of trade unions and the formation of a general confederation.

The first meeting was held in Sana'a between 10 and 12 April, 1984. Elections of the executive office of the confederation (7 members) took place in a free and democratic manner. Delegates from Arab and international labor organizations and unions attended the meeting. They helped in the formation of the confederation and expressed their desire to cooperate with it. Since its establishment, the General Confederation of Trade Unions carried out many cultural and labor-related activities on the local, Arab and international levels. Thanks to the care and support given by our national leadership, it achieved and continues to achieve its objectives. These objectives are:
- to create a spirit of cooperation and team work by material means and cultural activities for improving social relationships and placing them on higher ethical grounds;
- to eradicate illiteracy among the workers; to raise their educational and professional standard; to spread labor ethics among their ranks by holding forums, cultural and vocational courses conforming with public laws and the context of the NC;
- to strengthen cooperation between workers and employers, effectively carrying out the economic and social development plans;
- to regulate professional and industrial relations between the workers, departments and employers, and among workers themselves in such a way as to raise the worker's economic and social status;
- to organize training and educational programs aiming at the formation of a successful union leadership with a solid ethical base, serving the public good and preserving our Islamic faith;
- to increase and improve production and to maintain tools and machinery;
- to safeguard the rights and interest of the workers; to create cooperative societies; to provide any assistance and services fostering the social, health, cultural and economic standards of the workers and their families;
- to represent the workers in all labor organizations, be they Arab, regional or international, in conferences, symposiums and seminars;
- to allow workers of the republic to participate freely in the Arab and international trade union movement and to increase the effectiveness and the role of Yemeni workers in Arab and international unions.

In line with the democratic policy of our national leadership, many professional and specialized unions were established. The government willingly supported such mass organizations and assisted them in achieving their objectives by granting them the needed facilities. These unions include:
- Union of Yemeni Jurists
- Union of Yemeni Writers in both parts of Yemen, with branches in Sana'a, Taiz, Hodeidah and Ibb

- Union of Doctors and Pharmacists
- Union of Yemeni Engineers
- Union of Yemeni Journalists
- Union of Pilots and Aeronautic Navigators
- Union of Auxiliary Medical Occupations with branches in Sana'a, Taiz and Hodeidah
- Union of Agricultural Occupations
- Union of Artists
- Union of Economists
- Federation of Chambers of Commerce and its branches.

Each of these unions has its own objectives outlined in its bylaws. Objectives in common with other professional unions and societies included:
- raising the cultural and educational standard of the union's members and developing the profession by introducing modern methods and techniques;
- providing services which raise the social, health, cultural and economic levels of the members;
- caring for and safeguarding the rights and interests of the members;
- ensuring social solidarity among the members, extending help and care whenever necessary and in accordance with the articles of the bylaws;
- organizing general and specific educational and cultural courses and seminars;
- raising the general level of awareness in each professional area through newspapers, bulletins, magazines and periodicals;
- activating participation in the process of development according to the specialization of the union;
- representing the union and the profession in organizations on the Arab, regional and international levels.

The government also encouraged the formation of women's associations. There are now five such societies:
- Yemeni Women's Association, Sana'a
- Yemeni Women's Association, Taiz
- Yemeni Women's Association, Hodeidah
- Yemeni Women's Association, Ibb
- Yemeni Women's Association, Dhamar.

Each association has branches in the adjacent areas. They aim at developing the women's sector by combining their efforts and raising women's cultural and educational standards within the rights guaranteed by the Islamic Shari'ah, according to the famous words of the Prophet Muhammad: "women are the partners of men".

According to the bylaws of these associations, their main objectives are:
- to ensure that Yemeni women actively participate hand in hand with their male partners in accelerating the development of the Yemeni society;
- to foster the cultural, social and health awareness of the Yemeni women, enabling them to fully play their part in the service of society;
- to look into family matters in general and to attend to cases of maternity and childcare in particular;
- to promote women's activities in the fields of education and other sectors and to further their talents and capabilities;
- to participate in the drive against female illiteracy;
- to oppose bad and meaningless customs, to implant the principles of Islam and Islamic human values and to instill a patriotic consciousness in the hearts of the Yemeni women;
- to organize and conduct training, cultural and social courses and conferences dealing with women's affairs internally and externally.

The Yemeni Women's Association conducted and continues to conduct widespread activities in the quest for eradicating illiteracy, supporting education and advising on matters of maternity and childcare. It is receiving material and moral support from the government to carry out its important role in society.

In view of the importance of the cooperative societies in general and agricultural cooperatives in particular, preparations are currently underway to draw up a law which will be the framework for a Federation of Cooperative Societies. This federation will be established within the next few months.

Thus, the number of unions and associations has been increasing significantly during the era of the NC. They have expanded under the guidance of President Ali Abdullah Saleh, covering all classes and sectors of the society including workers, students, farmers, intellectuals, craftsmen and young people. These organizations have been joined by large numbers of our people everywhere.

Those mass organizations, which by now number more than three hundred, must perform their duties in all fields and make a concerted effort to achieve their objectives. They actively participate in building a better future for our beloved homeland by putting the contents of the NC into practice.

The next stage of development calls for the intensification of the role of the people in increasing production. One of the tasks shared by the PGC is to mobilize all forces, to utilize all potentials and to bring the people together in all walks of national life. Its main intent is to protect and immunize society against any infiltration which conflict with our Islamic belief, national unity and the principle of loyalty to the nation. This will also create an absolute belief in the Revolution and the Republic and safeguard our national sovereignty.

Successful democratic practices have hastened development and lead to the great success of democratic action, consolidating people's aspirations for building a bright new life. Our civilized, yet revolutionary option draws its meaning and value from Islam, encouraging the people to exercise all their national responsibilities. This is particularly significant in view of our democratic success, which shows itself in the creation of the elected legislative assembly of the PGC. Progress made by the PGC can be clearly perceived in the activities of its fourth general conference convened in November of 1988. This conference stressed broad popular participation in the course of democracy, development issues and Yemeni unity.

From the Holy Charter to the Permanent Constitution and the National Charter

by Dr. Ahmad Muhammad Al-Kibsi

Where are we now? This is a question that can be answered by historic facts and documents, making the difference apparent and testifying to change in Yemen for the better. The comparison between royalist and republican Yemen shows an immense divergence and provides the answer to our question: Where are we now? Yesterday's Yemen is unwanted - not just by the Yemenis - but by people everywhere.

The steps towards change are noticeable and we believe in continuation for the sake of realizing the hopes and aspirations of the Yemeni people. One of the most important steps is the building of a free democratic society ruled by constitutional institutions.

What was Yemen like prior to the outbreak of the 26 September Revolution of 1962? For the record, from the consensus of all those who visited Yemen it is apparent that the country was under absolute rule with all power concentrated in the hands of the Imam. Political participation and democratic institutions were lacking. It was a government where ties had been severed with the past and the present.

The violation of our heritage is represented by a clear and unquestionable offense to Islamic *shari'ah* which protects of the people's interests, safeguarding religion, life, property, peace of mind and future generations.

If one were to reflect upon the condition of the country prior to the September Revolution, one would find that the people whom the Islamic shari'ah and all divine laws sought to safeguard were actually completely devoid of human rights. Those who wish to study the human right situation during this period can refer to the regime's official newspapers to find a clear portrayal. [1]

The political system established by Imam Yahya Hamid Ad Din, extending from 1904 to 1962, witnessed the rule of three Imams: Yahya Hamid Ad-Din, the founder of the 20th century Yemeni state , Ahmad Yahya Hamid Ad-Din and Muhammad bin Ahmad bin Yahya Hamid Ad-Din. It was, as some historians asserted, one of the worst phases of Yemen's history. The political system was

characterized as follows:
- an absolute, individualist regime with all powers concentrated in the hands of the Imam;
- lack of political participation and institutions;
- absence of popular control;
- a break with tradition and isolation from the present.

If we wish to evaluate the system, we need to consider the goals the Imam wanted to realized by employing his power.

There is a vast difference between a ruler who concentrates power in his hands for the sake of mobilizing the resources of the country and accelerating the process of social and economic modernization and a ruler who concentrates all powers in his hands to perpetuate privileges for himself and his aids; thereby imposing a state of stagnation upon the development of the country.

There is also a difference between the ruler who imposes isolation upon his country for the sake of allowing it to depend upon its own resources and the ruler who imposes isolation to avoid development and isolate his country from a rapidly changing world.

There may appear certain similarities between the two types of regimes when observed from an external point of view. However, taking the respective aims and objectives into due consideration, the researcher has to make clear distinctions.

Evaluating the Imamate from the Viewpoint of Political Participation

In studying the political system prior to 1962, we cannot find any genuine public representation or legislative body. There was no organization allowing political participation except a very limited superficial one exercised by a minority close to the central ruler.

Moreover, the regime clearly disregarded Islamic political theory by transforming a system that was based on the election of the ruler by those entrusted with authority and responsibility to a hereditary one.

Imam Yahya, who came to power through election by those entrusted with authority and responsibility felt tempted to violate the rule that brought him to power and to transform it into a hereditary dynasty by creating the post of crown prince.

Imam Yahya took the following steps:
- he disregarded the *'ulama*, the "learned men" whom he feared as a threat to his power;

- he diminished the influence of the tribal sheikhs;
- he curtailed consultation and participation in government affairs;
- he discarded and prohibited the works of intellectuals and limited religious education;
- he created the position of crown prince.

These steps convinced the country's leaders of the corrupt nature of the Imam's government and made it an obligation to resist it. Various organizations emerged demanding reform and a return to the original *shurah* (consultation) system. When these attempts aiming to convince Imam Yahya of the need for reform and a return to shurah failed, the nationalist movements were founded. The first of these was the movement of the Free Yemenis in the 40ies, eventually leading to what can be called "the Revolution by the `ulama". The most important reasons leading to this revolution were:
- division within the ruling family itself;
- refusal of Imam Yahya to give up the policy of isolation, open up to the world and develop the country;
- conviction of some *'ulama* that change could only be helpful for the country;
- the on-going work of the nationalist movements and the demand for reform.

These factors, if added to the policy of suppression and total disregard for the wishes and hopes of the people, were bound to lead to dissatisfaction and rejection. The inevitable result was the 1948 Revolution. This was anticipated by the American diplomat Harlin Clark during his visit to Yemen and was included in his report to the State Department.

The Nationalist Movement and Its Demands

The call for shurah and parliamentary democracy has been associated with the nationalist movement since its inception in the mid-thirties of this century.

The nationalist movement aimed at reforming the country's deteriorating conditions by trying to give advice to the Imam. However, the Imam flatly disregarded all advice. The inevitable result was the conclusion by the leaders and members of the nationalist movement believed that there could be no alternative to revolution. This was the only way to stop the farce that was taking place in Yemen; thus the Constitutional Revolution was declared in February of 1948 demanding shurah and popular participation in all government affairs.

This is vividly expressed in the aims stated in the Holy National Charter:
- establishment of a representative system;
- improving social and economic conditions;

- purging of all elements corrupting the system;
- improving the overall condition of the army;
- ensuring freedom of opinion, speech, writing and association;
- terminating of the policy of isolation and the establishment of friendly relations with the civilized world. [2]

The President of the *Shurah* Council, son of the King of Yemen, against whom the revolution had taken place, declared to his supporters in Sana'a:

"We have sacrificed our positions for the sake of national reforms. We have trampled underfoot the power of the individual and disrupted the sway of tyranny. We have formulated for you higher ideals for the nation so that the Yemen can take its proper place among the nations of the world. You need to be consulted in dealing with your own affairs in obedience to Allah's eternal command:'Consult the people concerning their affairs.'"

"Esteemed citizens! You can see with your own eyes and hear with your own ears the difference between the era that Allah has ended leading the nation to the light of freedom and dignity, away from the era of keeping you in dungeons and prisons, destroying your minds. We are with you, leaders and princes. Neither power nor money will protect us as long as you are determined to correct our errors with your swords."

This revolution, however, was not successful owing to domestic circumstances as well as the nature of solidarity of the Arab states at that time, There was a silent agreement because they feared the principles espoused by the revolution, such as:
- rejection of the heir apparent which included rejection of hereditary rule;
- emphasis on the right of the people to participate in government decisions.

These principles contradicted the interests of the regimes in the Arab World at that time.

Even though the revolution was aborted and its leaders killed, its principles and aims remained alive in the minds of the educated youth. "The revolution left behind a question which the Yemenis continued to ponder for a long time. That question was: Why did all this occur in 1948? The people of Yemen tried to answer this question and staged various assassination attempts during the years 1955, 1958, 1959, 1960 and 1961. All of these attempts were finally crowned by the 1962 Revolution which overthrew the abhorrent religious regime. The republican system was established and the answer to the question became a tangible reality." [3]

The blood of the leaders of the 1948 Revolution became the flame held aloft by the youth of Yemen until achieving the goal long awaited on the 26th September of 1962 which marked the beginning of a totally different era and the starting point for building a new Yemen.

"If there was ever a country completely prepared for revolution and political change, it was none other than Yemen." [4]

Fifteen years earlier Harlin Clark had admitted: "Yemen is ready for change. That is the expressed conviction of the residents in cities and the countryside." [5]

The September Revolution became the historic opportunity for taking the Yemeni people out of a gloomy past, granting them the right to life, freedom and equality like other human beings. It was a humane revolution that returned to man his pride and dignity. It was a revolution against backwardness in all of its shapes and forms as declared in its six goals and reaffirmed by all successive legislation. It was also a revolution for political participation as specified by the fourth goal.

Even when the Revolution was facing its most critical times, confronting domestic and international conspiracies aiming at crushing it, the citizens were demanding a constitution, a Shurah Council and political institutions. The political leadership found itself facing numerous challenges such as the foundation of new political institutions, the preservation of national sovereignty and the realization of social and economic development.

Due to the difficult circumstances plaguing the country as a result of the burdensome heritage bequeathed by the defunct regime and due to difficult political conditions, the development of institutions was slow. The establishment of modern institutions meant an increase in state organs and organizations requiring the provision of qualified cadres. This was one of the most pressing challenges facing the revolutionary government which dispatched numerous missions abroad to prepare young people to take over these new tasks and responsibilities for the future of Yemen.

The Development of the New Political System

The development of the new political system took place in several stages. It was characterized by the emergence of trends and policies differing from those of the previous periods. A Constitutional Declaration was made on October 13, 1962, stating that all sovereignty was to rest with the people and not depend on the will of an individual ruler. Thus sovereignty was restored to its lawful owners, promising the realization of democracy for which the people had been struggling. It was to be a republican democracy, guaranteeing the rule of the people by the people.

Owing to the short period between the eruption of the revolution and this early Constitutional Declaration, those exercising sovereignty in the name of the people were not able to clarify the detailed structure of the government. They were content with mentioning general principles. The exercise of power during the transitional period was assigned to the Command Council and the Council of Ministers.

Eventually, the two councils were merged into a congress "that considers the state's general policy and subjects that pertain to it". In this manner a form of collective leadership was established.

This type of organization became necessary because of the extraordinary circumstances surrounding the Revolution. It was also needed for the sake of preparing a new constitution through the setup of a specialized committee. Its work in accordance with the Constitutional Declaration ended with the declaration of the Provisional Constitution on May 8, 1963. Even though this constitution had a time limit, its prologue affirms that the fifth goal of the Revolution is "the establishment of a representational system through which the sovereignty of the people is realized as the source of all power". The second article provides that "the Yemeni people are to rule themselves and are the source of all power in the state".

This Provisional Constitution did not take into account the organization of a legislative power. It furthermore did not refer to the formation of a representative council. Instead, legislative power was assigned to the Presidential Council and the President of the Republic. The Constitution did not clarify the manner of forming the Presidential Council, nor the exact number of its members. It also did not specify any conditions to be fulfilled by this Council. It did, however, empower the Council to dismiss members or admit new members to it. The importance of taking the constitutional oath before the President of the Republic was stressed and its members were prohibited from pursuing a second profession.

The Constitution was also limited by the time factor. The overall atmosphere of domestic and external conspiracies and the burdensome heritage of ignorance, poverty and disease inherited from the defunct regime had doubled the problems faced by the post-revolution government, yet the great objective, the declaration of the Provisional Constitution, which had been the focus of the people's struggle for so many years, was finally being fulfilled.

The mere creation of councils, of course, is not enough for establish democracy. The *Shura* Council, or parliament, has to be the legislative and control organ. It can only exercise its powers properly in a society that enjoys a certain degree of freedom.

The Constitution of 1963 was a provisional one. On April 27, 1964, the President of the Republic submitted a proposal for a Permanent Constitution. It was first submitted for "discussion and elaboration" and when "views on it had converged", it was promulgated.

This Permanent Constitution avoided some of the criticism that had been leveled at the Provisional Constitution. Article 48 stresses the necessity of an elected *Shura* Council made up of members chosen from among Yemeni notables and public figures. The number of members was fixed, and membership qualifications and the manner of appointment elaborated. However, how its members were to be chosen, whether through election or by appointment, was not clear. The

Council was to convene for three years from the date of its first session (Article 49).

The Permanent Constitution of 1964 must definitely be considered a step forward. It granted the Council (later to be known as the People's Constituent Assembly) the power of controlling the work of the executive and the right of questioning and casting a vote of no confidence against any of the ministers. The Council of Ministers was now placed under the control of the *Shura* Council, but even though this Constitution was not applied fully. It can, however, safely be considered a step forward, taking into account the situation in the Yemen Arab Republic at that time.

During the period from September 1964 till November 5, 1967, the country witnessed eight cabinet reshuffles. The average tenure of each cabinet during this period was only seven months. The Yemen Arab Republic also witnessed numerous popular congresses, each coming up with its own demands. The conditions prevailing during this stage have in fact determined the type of rule and policies that were to govern the country at later stages.

On previous occasions, it was stated that the 26 September Revolution was a revolution to build government institutions providing security for all citizens. The Revolution envisioned the creation of a state whose constitutional elements were to include the separation of powers, submission of rulers to the law, independence of the government from strong personalities, succession by legal means, establishment of citizens' individual rights and control of the ruling bodies by the legislative and judicial powers. It has previously been stated that a parliament, as a legislative and controlling power, cannot exist except in a society enjoying an appropriate degree of freedom. Owing to the exceptional circumstances the Yemen Arab Republic had experienced since its birth, none of the constitutions and constitutional declarations announced during that time were actually put into effect. The executive's domination of the other powers continued until national reconciliation between the contesting parties was achieved. Thereafter, legislative power moved from the plane of theory to that of practice albeit partially owing to the formation of a Provisional National Council that would exercise the functions of the *Shura* Council provided for under previous constitutions. This Council was also entrusted with the task of formulating a new Permanent Constitution for the country.

Government powers in the Yemen Arab Republic from then on, rested upon two primary documents: the country's Permanent Constitution (PC) and the National Charter (NC). Therefore it is important to understand the circumstances surrounding the emergence of these documents plus their characteristics and the liberties they guaranteed to the citizen.

Genesis of the 1970 Permanent Constitution

Among the major driving forces for the promulgation of the Permanent Constitution of 1970 was a successful reconciliation between the Yemeni factions that had previously opposed each other. This was achieved through the convention of several conferences. The Khamr Conference of 1965 witnessed a great gathering of Yemenis. Article 5 was among its most important decisions: "The conference endorses the demands raised by the great martyr, father of the Free Yemenis, Muhammad Mahmud al-Zubayri and his comrades in 1964". These fundamental demands were as follows:
- amendment of the Constitution;
- establishment of a Republican Council;
- formation of the *Shura* Council;
- declaration and foundation of a popular organization;
- formation of a national army;
- formation of a defense council;
- formation of a shari'ah court for trying people accused of squandering state funds and the people's resources.

The successful Corrective Movement of November 5, 1967 led to the formation of the Republican Council. [6] A number of important steps were taken, eventually leading to the Permanent Constitution of 1970.

Among them was the issuing of Republican Council Resolution No. 38 of 1968 on the formation of a Founding Committee made up of fifteen members from among senior state leaders, scholars, intellectuals and those entrusted with responsibility and power. Article 2 of this resolution determined the two principal tasks of this committee as being the preparation of a draft Permanent Constitution and the preparation for the formation of the *Shura* Council determining its scope and competence. [7]

And even though the Founding Committee did commence the work assigned to it, the political leadership deemed it necessary to form another provisionally appointed national council representing all popular segments to undertake this task and take the function of a legislative body for the country until the election of a *Shura* Council.

In 1968, Provisional Constitutional Decree No. 2 regarding the Provisional National Council and the preparation of the country's constitution was passed. Article 2 provided that "the Provisional National Council be responsible for the formulation of the Constitution of the Yemen Arab Republic".

Thus, the powers and tasks of the Founding Committee were assigned to the Provisional National Council, which was also entrusted with exercising legislative functions until the emergence of an elected *Shura* Council.

Methods of formulating constitutions vary. There is the monarchical or undemocratic method represented by the royal decree or royal ruling. Democratic methods for formulating a constitution are the employment of a founding assembly or the conducting of a popular referendum.

As for the Permanent Constitution of the Yemen Arab Republic which was promulgated in 1970, the Provisional National Council undertook the following steps: [8]

First, a preparatory committee was formed whose members were distinguished by their knowledge, sound opinion and wisdom, with the aim of preparing a draft permanent constitution, thus completing what had been commenced by the earlier Founding Committee. After numerous meetings and discussions, the committee was able to submit a draft constitution compatible with the principles and values of Yemeni society.

The draft Permanent Constitution was then submitted by the preparatory committee to the Provisional National Council for study, evaluation and eventual endorsement. The Provisional National Council approved the draft Permanent Constitution, but refrained from discussion, study and expression of views on its articles and provisions, leaving that to the people on the grounds that the people are the source of all power and they alone have the right to do so. The draft was submitted to the people "with the people having full freedom to discuss, evaluate and express opinions on each and every article of the draft."

Three months elapsed before the Constitution was finally formulated on the evening of September 26, 1970. During this period meetings were held to consult with the various segments of society in the capital, the towns and the villages. Open dialogue was conducted with citizens and views exchanged.

The Republican Council received cables and letters expressing the views of citizens. It met with theologians and scholars, sheikhs and intellectuals and listened to them.

There were certain shortcomings in the methods used to know the views of the people concerning the Permanent Constitution. It was limited to an attempt to ascertain the views of some social segments on a narrow basis and through unprecedented means not accessible by the majority of the Yemeni people.

Yet, there were genuine manifestations of a democratic *shura* orientation on part of the political leadership. The people were requested to participate in the formulation of the Permanent Constitution and the potential of the people to participate in the democratic process in an intelligent manner was taken into consideration . The manner of formulating the 1970 Permanent Constitution was rather close to the established democratic methods for preparing constitutions.

The Genesis of the National Charter

The September Revolution was not an end in itself. The Yemeni people embarked upon it with the aim of destroying the Imamic regime, pulling themselves out of the Middle Ages, and joining the prosperous civilization of the 20th Century.

In order to realize the revolutionary aspirations of the Yemeni people by transferring the aims of the September Revolution into practical reality, the wise political leadership, represented by Colonel Ali Abdullah Saleh, deemed it necessary to find "...a practical formula that interacts with their principles, values and aims of their revolution".[9]

In order to preserve national unity and fill the political vacuum from which Yemen had suffered, it was imperative that "...there should be a National Charter containing the thoughts and ideas which all sons of the Yemeni people agree upon, and thus ensure intellectual freedom and protection from political bondage, deprivation and division".[10]

The preparatory stage was characterized by the following steps:[11]
- The political leadership delegated the task of formulating concepts for a National Charter to the People's Constituent Assembly.
- A committee was formed, including various well-known personalities from within and outside the People's Constituent Assembly. Other sub-committees were created that included representatives of certain social layers. Meetings, discussions and seminars were organized.
- All these efforts resulted in the drafting of the National Charter which was submitted to the President, who in turn referred it to the Advisory Council for discussion; the draft was expanded and made a more comprehensive one.
- With the aim of arriving at an even more comprehensive draft, the political leadership decided that it was necessary to have it further discussed by an expanded meeting attended by the members of the Council of Ministers, the Advisory Council, the governors of the provinces and other officials from the popular, civil and military establishment. All those in attendance voted for the draft to be submitted to the people.

Because of the political leadership's belief in the necessity for popular participation, and because of their willingness to enable the people to express their thoughts, hopes and aspirations freely, "Republican Decree No. 5 of 1980 was promulgated regarding the formation of a National Dialogue Committee to prepare for the General Peoples Congress..."[12]

The National Dialogue Committee was composed of "fifty members from among sincere patriotic elements representing all segments of the people in our country. The task of this committee was to present and explain the draft Charter to the people. Views were to be exchanged with the public by means of dialogue..."[13]

The National Dialogue Committee undertook the task of presenting the draft National Charter to the people who should have a decisive say in determining the affairs of their political, economic, social and cultural life.

The National Dialogue Committee took "...about two years of internal discussion. Then came the stage of presenting the draft to the people in order to ascertain their views. The final result came only after the completion of public dialogue, where everyone participated in a constructive and responsible manner under the supervision of the members of the Dialogue Committee. This was carried out by way of a plebiscite. The completed forms carrying the views of each citizen were returned to the Committee. The Committee sifted, categorized and allocated these views to the various chapters of the Charter as directed by the President. Considering the opinions expressed by the population, the draft Charter was reformulated.[14]

After the National Dialogue Committee had presented the draft NC to the people through public meetings, the political leadership opened the way for the election of a People's Congress. Resolution No. 19 of 1981 was issued determining the number of members of the People's General Congress to be one thousand representatives. 70% of the representatives were to be freely elected by the people and 30% were to be appointed by the state. Their task was to revise again the draft NC in the light of the contents of the questionnaires and to adopt its final formulation and determine the manner of its application.

Among the resolutions and recommendations of the first People's General Congress were the following:

- The Conferees unanimously adopted the NC in its final version considering it to be the intellectual framework for patriotic work after having added some amendments that had emerged during the convention of the Congress.
- The representatives confirmed their adherence to the National Charter in spirit and letter and took it upon themselves to follow up on its implementation, each representative within the scope of his mandate.
- The Congress underlined the obligation of all government organs, public establishments and institutions and all citizens to apply the NC in their spheres of work, plans, programs and working methods.[15]

The Congress also approved the existence of the People's General Congress including its various components and its continuation as a political organization applying the provisions of the National Charter.

The Principles of the Permanent Constitution and the National Charter

Both the PC and the NC adopted the concept of a limited government. In Article 65, the Constitution explicitly states that "the *Shura* Council has the right to withdraw confidence from the government..."

The Constitution not only granted the *Shura* Council the right of withdrawing confidence from the government, but also empowered the Supreme Constitutional Court, which is also elected by the people, to try every member of the executive branch. Paragraph (c) of Article 155 provides that the Supreme Constitutional Court has the right "to try the Chairman and members of the Presidential Council, the Prime Minister and the ministers."

Similarly, we find the National Charter adopting the concept of limited government which is responsible to the representatives of the people. When speaking of democracy, the NC underlines that "our democracy rejects the idea of concentrating power in the hands of an individual or a group of individuals. Rather, it should be delegated to constitutional institutions represented by the legislative power of the *Shura* Council acting on behalf of the people and the executive power represented by the government which is responsible to the *Shura* Council."

Further clarifying in what way the government is responsible to the *Shura* Council, the Charter stipulates that the *Shura* Council has the right "...to grant or withhold confidence in the government, and has the right to hold the government accountable as a whole or any minister participating in it."[16]

Sovereignty of the People

Sovereignty of the People means the right of the people to rule themselves as their own master. The Permanent Constitution and the National Charter made the people the source of all sovereignty and power. The Constitution states that "the people are the source of power."[17]

As for the National Charter, it acknowledges the sovereignty of the people in clarifying the concept of democracy. This is a fundamental Islamic rule based on *shura*, mutual consultation and the right of the people to chose their rulers.[18]

Furthermore, the National Charter elaborates on democracy as "the state with its various powers being a right of the people, and therefore, the people being the source of all power." Similarly, the National Charter underlines that the people are the only reference in all such matters.

Separation of and Cooperation between Powers

The principle of the separation of powers ensures that no individual or group of individuals can impose their arbitrary will on the destiny and capabilities of the people. This separation of powers represents one of the most fundamental principles of democracy. The PC makes an implicit point of reference concerning the separation of and cooperation between powers.

The NC was more explicit than the PC in adopting the principle of the separation of powers. It stresses that "...our republican system is a representative democratic one embodied in the various constitutional institutions. It is based on the principle of the separation of powers and clarifies and details the competence of each power, aspects of cooperation and coordination between the legislature and the executive, and how laws are to be safeguarded by a sound judiciary."

Ways of cooperation between powers, especially between the legislature and executive, are laid down in the articles of the PC and the text of the NC. The executive acts to serve the legislature. Services include:
- preparation for and supervision of the elections of the *Shura* Council, which is the supreme legislative power of the state;[19]
- the right of appointment of 20% of the total number of members of the *Shura* Council, which numbers 159 members;[20]
- the right to call upon the *Shura* Council to convene;[21]
- the right to dissolve the *Shura* Council;[22]
- the right to propose laws and amendments to laws and express views on them, and eventually approve and promulgate them after their adoption by the *Shura* Council;[23]

On the other hand, the PC and the NC grant the legislature various rights that directly influence the executive. Among these rights are:
- the right of the *Shura* Council members to question the government and government officials and level charges against them;[24]
- undertake the nomination and election of the President of the Republic;[25]
- the right of the *Shura* Council to withdraw its confidence from the government.[26]

From the preceding review and a reading of the articles of the 1970 PC and the text of the NC we can conclude that both the Constitution and the Charter have adopted the principle of separation of and cooperation between powers. Each branch has been given certain rights enabling it to independently fulfill its tasks on the one hand while cooperating with the other branches where necessary.

Characteristics of the Permanent Constitution and the National Charter

Certain characteristics distinguish the PC from the NC, while other characteristics are in common.

Affirmation of Adherence to the Dictates of the Islamic Creed

The PC underlines the need to abide by the dictates of the Islamic creed. It provides in Article 2 that "Islam is the religion of the state." It goes on to clarify: "The Islamic creed is the source of all laws."

As for the NC, it sets aside a whole chapter under the title: "Islam - the Creed and the Law". Thus, the reader of the provisions of the NC will find that it has an Islamic orientation and is based upon Islamic principles.

The Charter states that "Islam for the Yemeni people was and still is the basis of their intellectual and spiritual constitution. With its moral principles and values Islam has become the conscience of our people. It is impossible to disregard it or replace it with anything else since the Islamic concept of creation of the universe and man is distinguished by its comprehensiveness in all aspects of material and spiritual life". [27]

The Charter also rejects any un-Islamic orientation. It states: "We reject any theory of rule or economy or politics or sociology that is contradictory to our Islamic creed and law." [28]

Striving to Realize Yemeni National Unity

Strengthening and restoring of Yemeni unity is the principle goal for which the people are still striving to realize. Both, the PC and the NC have articulated this great and sacred popular aim.

It is for this reason that the Constitution states that "Yemen is an indivisible whole and the struggle for the realization of Yemeni unity is the sacred duty of every citizen." [29]

Article 5 of the PC recognizes the Yemeni citizens' struggle for the realization of a united homeland. This is considered a sacred duty. In fact, the popular desire of the Yemeni people to restore unity has surpassed official statements concerning the matter. The PC reminds us that the activities of the masses are more profound than official moves in realizing higher national and pan-Arab aims.

The NC considers comprehensive Yemeni unity, one of the achievements of ancient Yemeni civilization. This is expressed through the statement: "Our people could not have created their ancient civilization without stability, security and peace. This was achieved through the unity of the land, the people and the government." [30]

In reply to the question, "Why is national unity necessary?" the NC affirms: "National unity provides the strength with which we confront all dangers that threaten our entity, stability and national sovereignty." [31]

The NC maintains that Yemeni unity represents the inevitable strategic aim for people's progress and development, enabling Yemen to take on a positive and effective role on the pan-Arab and international levels. It states: "Yemeni unity is the destiny of our people in the north and in the south of the homeland, imperative for their complementary growth and development. It is also the guarantee of their ability to defend territorial integrity and of their ability to play an effective and positive role on the pan-Arab and international levels." [32]

Affirmation of Arabism by Relation and Unity

Both the PC and the NC underline the Arab origins of the Yemeni people, of their civilization and history.

The Introduction of the PC expresses this fact by stating: "We Yemenis are an Arab Muslim people. We can have no existence for ourselves or for our homeland without taking account of our Arab roots. No people belonging to the same race can claim to be of earlier origin than us or try to teach us lessons concerning Arabism." [33]

Furthermore, the PC states in Article 1: "Yemen is a fully sovereign, independent Islamic Arab state. It is a representative revolutionary democracy and the Yemeni people are a part of the Arab World."

Similarly, the NC affirms the Yemeni people's Arab identity and the need to seek the realization of comprehensive Arab unity. It states: "Since our link with the Arab world is part of our destiny, we must continue serious interaction to implement the wishes and aspirations of the Arab World." [34]

The NC also underlines the firm belief of the Yemeni people in Arab unity, interaction with its issues and concerns and its just and legitimate causes. It states: "Our belief in Arab unity is affirmed through partaking in all of the just and legitimate causes of our Arab world ... and through our contribution to all battles against our common enemies." [35]

Prohibition of Partisanship

The Permanent Constitution permits the establishment of associations and trade unions by guaranteeing "the freedom to form associations and trade unions on a sound national foundation is ensured in accordance with the terms and conditions defined by law". Yet, it clearly rejects partisanship in all of its forms. Article 37 of the Constitution stresses: "Partisanship in all of its forms is prohibited."

The NC does not take a firm and decisive stand on the issue of partisanship. Concerning reference in the NC to loyalty to the homeland and the preservation of national unity, there is a requirement that earlier loyalty previously given because of communal, lineal, tribal or party affiliation and other ties that counter national unity and adversely affect the interests of the citizen and the homeland must now be given to the state. [36]

The NC considers that "...any material or intellectual subservience to a foreign organization is treason and damaging to the higher interests of the homeland and a violation of national loyalty." [37]

As a matter of fact, the PC is more explicit and frank than the NC in its reference to the prohibition of partisanship.

Statement of Public Freedoms and Rights in the Permanent Constitution and the National Charter

In order for the citizen to play a proper role he must not be deprived of his rights and liberties as stated in both divine laws as well as international agreements. Among these rights and liberties are the right to life, the right to security, the right and freedom of creed and religion, the freedom of opinion and expression, the right to possession and ownership, the right to work as well as other rights and liberties.

Both the PC and the NC ensure the Yemeni citizen many of these rights and liberties.

The Principle of Equality

Aiming at the founding a strong, cohesive Yemeni society the PC stresses the need to realize justice, freedom and equality between the members of society.

It considers that "social solidarity based on justice, freedom and equality is the foundation of society." It further clarifies in Article 19, "All Yemenis are equal with regard to their rights and public duties."

The NC similarly adopts the concept of comprehensive equality among the people by stating, "There shall be no sovereignty because of lineage or individual, membership to particular sects or groups. All citizens combined form a single organism drawing life from each member and granting life to each member." [38]

As for further details concerning the principles of equality, the Charter underlines that "citizens are equal when casting votes, expressing views and in all rights and duties. All have the right to participate in public activities, the right to enjoy political and civil rights, the right to be eligible as well as to vote. These are all rights that must be ensured to both individuals and groups equally and they should be realized in a democratic manner, placing the national interest above every other consideration." [39]

Thus, we find that the NC ensures all Yemenis, individuals and groups the right to exercise civil and political rights, provided that this is done by democratic means and that the higher interests of the homeland are placed above every other consideration.

The Individual's Personal and Material Rights and Liberties

The right to life, security, freedom of movement, place of living and secrecy of communications are the most important rights and liberties that the individual must obtain.

That is why we find both the PC and the NC ensuring each Yemeni citizen personal rights and liberties.

The PC guarantees the right to life and security by affirming that "blood, property and honor are sacrosanct and both the be a good and effective shari'ah and the law ensure the means of their protection". [40] Similarly, the Constitution states, "Prisoners cannot be physically or mentally tortured." [41] The Constitution further underlines that the "accused is innocent until proven guilty and there shall be no punishment except after a legitimate trial where procedures are regulated by law with the right of defense being guaranteed." [42]

Ensuring the sanctity of residence, the Constitution provides that "dwellings are sanctified and cannot be kept under surveillance nor entered without the permission of their owners except in instances detailed by the law." [43]

Similarly, the Constitution does not permit the expulsion of any Yemeni citizen from his homeland, nor a ban on his return to it. In the event of the arrest, inspection or detention of any citizen, such acts must be carried out in accordance with the law and undertaken by an authority empowered by the law. "It shall not be permissible to expel a Yemeni from Yemeni territory or bar his return to it. It is also not permissible to arrest, detain or inspect any citizen except under the law and by an authority empowered by the law." [44]

Concerning the secrecy of communications the Constitution underlines that "the freedom of postal, cable and telephone communications and their secrecy is ensured. It shall not be permissible to supervise such communications nor disclose their contents or delay them, except in instances determined by law." [45]

Similarly, we find the NC at pains to ensure that the Yemeni citizen enjoys all personal and material rights and liberties, be these the right to life, security, movement or the freedom of residence, choice of work or security from oppressive detention. It "ensures freedom of movement, freedom to select employment and the freedom of every citizen to chose a dwelling and to remain in his homeland. He shall not be unjustly transgressed upon nor killed nor have his property plundered. His dwelling shall not be entered except with his permission. He shall not be subjected to surveillance and inspection nor charged on suspicion and must be protected from oppressive detention."

The National Charter continues with the enumeration of the citizen's personal rights, emphasizing that arrest and imprisonment should be a means left to the judiciary alone. It underlines further that the accused must be informed of the charges being brought against him and be given the opportunity to defend himself. It also prohibits concealment of the citizen's whereabouts from his relatives and family and further prohibits the use of physical and mental torture against the citizen, no matter what the causes or justifications may be. [46]

The Individual's Moral Rights and Liberties

The freedom of creed, worship, opinion, expression, association, education and the press are among the most important freedoms and rights ensured and adopted by both the PC and the NC for all Yemeni citizens.

The Constitution underlines the freedom of creed and worship and human rights in a general way as stated in Article 43 pointing out that "it is not permissible for the state to discriminate in human rights by virtue of religion, color, sex, language, profession or nationality."

The Constitution in this preceding article provides for equality between human beings in general regarding basic human rights, no matter of what race, religion, nationality, color or profession they may be.

Moreover, the PC underlines the sanctity of places of worship, considering them to be an extension of the freedom of religion. This has been extended to cover places of learning with the aim of ensuring scientific and academic freedom. It states: "Places of worship and learning have a sanctity that cannot be transgressed, except in specific instances made imperative by security needs as specified by the law." [47]

Concerning the freedom of opinion and speech, the Constitution provides that "each citizen has the right to express in speech or writing or photography his thinking within the limits of the law". [48]

The Constitution also clarifies the freedom of association by providing that "the individual has the right of association without need of permission or prior notice. Public meetings, processions and gatherings are allowed in accordance with the terms and conditions laid out by the law." [49]

For its part, the NC underlines the citizen's moral rights and liberties, making it a condition that the citizen exercise them within the framework of the Charter. Thus, regarding freedom of thought, the Charter provides that "freedom of expression of opinion or thought through various means must be ensured".

Freedom of opposition is granted by the NC on condition that its exercise must be by democratic means and that it must aim at the preservation of the higher national interests. The Charter states: "...the freedom of opposition must be ensured for individuals and groups on an equal basis, to be exercised by democratic means, placing the national interest above every other consideration..." [50]

The Individual's Social and Economic Rights and Liberties

The right and freedom of work, the right of ownership and social justice are among the most important individual rights and liberties in the social and economic sphere.

Both the PC and the NC point to the need of the Yemeni citizen to obtain these rights and liberties and to enjoy them if he is expected to contribute substantially to the modernization and comprehensive development process aiming at catching up with contemporary human civilization and matching the progress that other countries have achieved.

The Constitution is explicit in underlining the right and liberty of every Yemeni to work within the context of the law: "Each citizen has the right to do the work of his choice within the limits of the law. No compulsory work shall be imposed upon anyone, except under conditions set out by the law in the public interest and against a just remuneration." [51]

As for the Yemeni citizen's pursuit of private economic activities and the right of ownership, the PC endorses this right, provided that it does not undermine the public interest. In the event private property is sequestrated in the interests of society, its owner has the right to obtain just compensation. The Constitution clarifies that "private ownership is ensured and private property cannot be seized except in the public interest. The law determines the amount and manner of compensation." [52]

As for the right to social justice, the Constitution states in more than one article, and specifically in Article 6 that "social solidarity based on justice, freedom and equality is the basis of society". In Article 15 it says that "social justice and the public interest are the basis for taxation and public expenditure."

The Constitution also stresses that every citizen is entitled to receive health care: "Health care is the right of all Yemenis, ensured by the State through the founding of various hospitals and health establishments and the expansion of services is to be carried out in accordance with available resources." [53]

The NC pursues the same line in specifying the rights and liberties of the Yemeni citizen on social and economic levels. It clarifies the concept of social justice, the right to work and the citizen's right of free choice of work according to his inclinations and capabilities. He should not be compelled to undertake any work, except if warranted by the interests of society and provided that this should not violate the provisions of the merciful Islamic shari'ah.

"It is social justice that the doors to work should be open, so that the citizen may choose what he is qualified for by his inclination, experience and competence. A specific job should not be imposed upon him except if such is warranted in the interests of society as a whole. Citizens should not be barred from work opportunities, except if such employment should be in contravention to the provisions of the Islamic Sha'ria." [54]

The right to private ownership is expressed by the NC in more than one place. Economic democracy must be practiced in accordance with specific fundamentals, among them "... non-exploitation, prohibition of price hikes and monopolies except in the public interest and with just compensation, equality of citizens before the law, firmly prohibiting the exploitation of the weak or of the deprived. This is regulated by Islamic morality which prohibits usury, exploitation, monopoly, cheating and every other form of unlawful gain. There shall be no sovereignty of class over class; neither shall there be any usurpation of power by one people excluding others." [55]

The NC provides a general concept of ownership, clarifying that "...the ownership that we approve and safeguard is that which follows the purpose of Islam, is legitimately established and has a legitimate movement." [56] Thus, we find the NC adopting and respecting private ownership as long as it is not incompatible with the public interest. The unlawful practices of private ownership such as price hikes, exploitation, monopoly, cheating and usury must not only be resisted but destroyed with the aim of realizing social justice and spreading equality, love and fraternity among the people of one single society.

Again affirming the right of the Yemeni citizen to lawful private property and ownership, the Charter reads: "Lawful private ownership is ensured and private property cannot be seized except under the provisions of the law in the public interest and with just compensation." [57]

When dealing with the social rights of the Yemeni citizen, the NC underlines the need for the prevalence of social justice. Social justice among the members of society means "that the individual is protected from oppression, subjugation and economic exploitation. Suitable conditions should be created enabling every individual to make full use of his qualifications and potential." [58]

In conclusion it can be said that the NC aims at spreading social peace, creating a strong Yemeni society under the prevalence of love, cooperation and harmony. "Social life means cooperating and complementing each other, releasing constructive private and public energies. It does not mean conflict and quarrel among classes." [59]

Councils and Assemblies

Since the promulgation of the PC, the Republic has seen three representative councils and assemblies. Two of these were elected ones, namely the *Shura* Councils of 1971 and of 1988. The Peoples' Constituent Assembly of 1978 - 1988 came into being by appointment. The country has also seen a period during which there was no council at all, from October 1975 till February 1978.

The 1971 *Shura* Council was the first elected council in the country since the outbreak of the 26 September Revolution in 1962. The PC assigned to it the task of legislative authority. Article 44 provides that "the *Shura* Council is the supreme legislative body of the state". The Council is made up of 159 democratically elected members. The law regulates elections and the conditions for becoming a member of the Council. The President of the Republic appoints 20% of the members (Article 46). Thus the country is divided into 128 electoral districts, while the head of state can appoint an additional 31 members.

The PC and the Election Law specify the conditions for candidacy. The candidate must be a Yemeni of not less than 25 years of age. He must not be illiterate and be of good character and uphold Islamic tenets. He must not be previously convicted of a felony and he must be honorable and respectable. He cannot not be a civil servant.

It can be said that the conditions required from the candidate are the same as those potential electorates must also fulfill. Differences concern only age and education. The voter must not be less than 18 years of age and must be able to read and write.

The parliamentary term has been determined to be four years by Article 50 of the PC. The term commences from the council's first meeting. The same Article provides that new elections must be held within sixty days prior to the end of the parliamentary term. During these sixty days, elections are to be held and their results declared, thus the formation of the new Council is completed before the old one ends.

In case elections are postponed for any reason, the old Council is to continue to function until a new one has been elected, but this extension should not exceed three months. Should it be necessary to extend this period as well, owing to unfavorable conditions for holding elections, a law must be promulgated determining such an additional extension.

The *Shura* Council of 1971

The 1971 *Shura* Council did not function until the end of its term. It began the term in the era of the Presidential Council. In June 1974 it was frozen for a period of five months by the Command Council and the people were not called upon to elect a new Council. It was not given the opportunity to complete its legal term which ended in October 1975. The Council was virtually dissolved. This aroused the anger of many leading personalities in the country who participated in the second Khamr conference and condemned the dissolution of the Council, calling for new elections. Other conferences were organized in support of the dissolution and sent cables to the Command Council supporting its decisions.

The Council never occupied the prominent position assigned to it within the political system or in the decision-making process. Despite all the efforts exerted by the Council, it never functioned as the main legislature or as a symbol of the people's power and sovereignty. This may have been caused by the lack of competence and capability of many of its members and the absence of material and moral support. However, it should be remembered that the Council was a correct step on the road towards democracy even though it was formed during a period when the country was engrossed in domestic conflicts and facing international conspiracies. There was also a gross lack of resources and scarcity of qualified cadres.

The People's Constituent Assembly

In his opening speech to the People's Constituent Assembly, the late President Ahmad Al-Ghashmi stated that the most severe mistake committed by the previous political system was the "freezing of democratic life by deactivating the *Shura* Council". After his assumption of office, he lost no time in founding the People's Constituent Assembly as a preparatory step paving the way for full democratic parliamentary life. He issued the Constitutional Declaration of February 6, 1978, on the formation of the People's Constituent Assembly consisting of 99 members who were chosen by the Command Council. Its most important function was to determine the form of state leadership, adopt measures to put them into effect and fulfill the tasks of the *Shura* Council.

The Assembly undertook the tasks assigned to it and decided to change the post of head of state from a Presidential Council to a individual President representing the unity of the homeland.

History will record the decisive and important role which this Assembly played during the crisis preceding President Ahmad Al-Ghashmi's assassination. The Assembly successfully foiled all plans by various enemies. This will remain a lasting achievement even though the Council did not play any other major role.

Following the election of Col. Ali Abdullah Saleh by the People's Constituent Assembly as the new President of the Republic, the Assembly's membership was increased to 159 and new tasks were assigned to it. It now had to undertake most of the tasks of the *Shura* Council provided for by the Constitution. During its subsequent parliamentary term the Assembly played an important role in national politics and in the preparation for the election of the *Shura* Council in July 1988.

The *Shura* Council of 1988

The *Shura* Council is clearly different from previous councils. It came into being during a period of political stability and awareness. The conditions and circumstances surrounding Yemen in 1988 were quite different from those of 1968, 1971 and 1978. The People's Constituent Assembly, even though appointed, played a clear and prominent role in preparing the country for general and free elections of a political organization which did not exist prior to 1982 or prior to the *Shura* Council. The *Shura* Council is both a legislative and a controlling body. Legislation has its source in Islam, the Holy Book and the Prophet's Traditions and the Council functions on this very basis. Islam is a religion suited to every place and time. Legal judgments are deducted from the detailed tenants of the Holy Book and the Traditions of the Prophet.

The Council also establishes regulations for domestic and international relations if there is no clarification in either the Holy Book or the Traditions. Such legislation may become necessary in response to the requirements of a different place or time. Needs change just as desires change. Islamic legislation remains binding for all Yemeni people throughout history. In addition, there is a need for organizing and regulating all matters of life through the capable and efficient use of all modern technology and other achievements. Qualified and capable Yemeni progress and uplift the country. The Council also exists in order to exercise control over the executive in the quest for progress.

It will be noted from the PC, the NC and the statements of the political leadership that the Council has been given all powers to pursue its work in a manner that serves the good of the people. This is being achieved by sound opinions and thus providing just government.

Elections

According to the PC and Law No. 29 of 1980, the *Shura* Council should number 159 members who should be elected in general and free elections with the exception of 20% to be appointed by the President of the Republic.

Electorates

Law No. 1 of 1971 concerning the *Shura* Council has adopted the principle of dividing the country into several electorates. The principle of equality was maintained by taking the number of citizens as the criteria for such divisions. Law No. 8 of 1975 determined the districts to number 128, each district electing one representative. The High Election Committee is concerned with the exact division of electoral districts taking into consideration the principle of equality between citizens. Article 24 allows for the population of a given district to exceed the prescribed number by 10%. Law No. 29 of 1980 adhered to the provisions of previous legislation.

The Electoral System

The members of the 1971 *Shura* Council were elected indirectly on the basis of a system of stratification from village to sub-district to district levels. However, this was amended by Law No. 29 of 1980 which called for direct elections. Article 26 provides for elections through direct and equal balloting.

Preparations for Elections

Preparations are carried out by the entry of the voters' names in the electoral lists after detailing the terms, conditions and measures of nomination. The President of the Republic directed the People's Constituent Assembly to make preparations for the election of the *Shura* Council which it did ensuring the correct selection of representatives by the people. Beginning in March 1988, the process of voters' registration started in a precise manner after completing the division of the country into 128 electoral districts. The citizens were then divided among the electoral districts in accordance with the 1986 population census which put the country's population at 9,274,173 persons. Each electoral district comprised some 72,000 citizens. The Supervisory Committee of the Assembly determined polling stations within each electoral district in accordance with population density and the area surrounding the electoral district. The registration of voters continued throughout March. 1,110,300 voters, some 10% of the population, were finally registered in the end. This is considered to be an appropriate number in view of the fact that nearly half of the population are children and a large number of citizens live abroad as emigrants. Moreover the female part of the population does not participate in politics, due to prevailing social conditions. It will be noted that in Yemen, political awareness seems to be greater than in other, similar countries that went through a comparative electoral experience.

A presidential decree determined the election day to be July 5, 1988. 1,293 candidates competed for the 128 available seats.

The Election Day and Results

When on the morning of the 5th of July the voters went out to the polling stations to elect 128 representatives to the *Shura* Council, they were opening a new stage in their political lives characterized by active campaigning and competition.

Armed with a new sense of confidence, citizens were allowed to select their representatives in full liberty. The President of the Republic directed the people to abide by their conscience in the process of selection. He summarized the conditions that must be met by the candidates, specifically their "belief in Allah and our country. Our people are known for their faith in Allah, in the Revolution and in the republican system. This is in addition to their loyalty to the homeland, their honesty, selflessness and modesty."

Long queues lined up before the polling stations. Everything proceeded smoothly and calmly. The government did well by staying away from the electoral process. At the end of the day, the supervisors opened the ballot boxes and began with the count of votes in the presence of the candidates who had to sign the minutes of the process, leaving each other and the people fully convinced in the soundness of the elections.

Numerous international news media have testified to the cleanness of the elections. As a matter of fact, the government in the past did not always stay clear of the actual election process, be it for the elections to the People's General Congress, the Local Councils, the General Congress or other elections. This time, however, there was no direct government interference whatsoever. No ballot boxes were changed or burnt, no citizen was prevented from casting his vote and no crisis was fabricated at any voting center.

There was a high turnout at the election with long queues of voters lining up in front of the polling stations. Different elements of society made it into the Council. The results also reflected the variables of education, age and occupation upon the composition of the Council. A number of educated youth, experts in various fields and other professionals succeeded in winning office.

After the appointment of the 31 members by the President of the Republic, the Council's membership includes academics, professional politicians, religious personalities, tribal sheikhs, military men, intellectuals, farmers, merchants and contractors. We also find that both young and elderly people are represented. Such a composition, in fact, is well suited to represent the whole of Yemen.

Internal Regulations of the Council

For members of the Council to be able to fulfill their tasks, it is necessary that guarantees exist enabling them to fulfill their responsibilities in full liberty and independence. Perhaps the most important of these guarantees is the right to hold meetings throughout the prescribed term of four years including meetings which are either ordinary or extra-ordinary ones.

The PC has granted the Council the right and the power to enact its own internal rules, namely regulations governing the way in which the Council works and the committees which it appoints (Article 60). These regulations not only pertain to the way of working, but also determine the Council's chairmanship, secretariat, committees and the competence of each.

At its first meeting the Council elects by absolute majority a chairman, two deputy chairmen and a secretary general from among the Council members for the parliamentary term. The chairman chairs the Council meetings, which he opens and regulates, determines the order of the speakers and the subjects for discussion. He also presents suggestions to the Council, announces the resolutions of the Council and closes meetings. The chairman represents the Council and speaks on its behalf in communicating with other organizations.

During the newly elected Council's first meeting, candidates were nominated to the post of chairman, deputy chairmen and secretary general. Elections were held by secret ballot and Qadhi Abdulkarim Al-Arashi was elected chairman of the *Shura* Council by an absolute majority of votes. The new Council chairman is well-known for his political acumen and experience. He had previously acted as chairman of the People's Constituent Assembly. He was also chairman of the Presidential Council following the assassination of the previous President of the Republic. The Council also elected Mr. Said Al Hakimi and Mr. Yusuf Ash-Shahari deputy chairmen and Mr. Ali Muqbil Ghuthaym secretary general. All three are well-known for their competence and capability.

The secretariat is composed of the chairman, the two deputy chairmen and the secretary general. It supervises the activities of the Council and the committees to ensure a smooth work routine. During periodic meetings the secretariat determines important subjects that are to be submitted to the Council for discussion.

Committees have been formed for drafting legislation and work has been divided among them according to specialization. The committees are of great importance to the Council. They concentrate upon specific subjects, going into great detail and depth. Each member has been given the liberty of joining the committee(s) that he considers himself capable of contributing to. The activities of the representatives are best evaluated by observing the committees in action. There, specialized and detailed discussions are taking place, much more so than in the plenary sessions.

The permanent committees constitute the heart of the Council. In their fields of specialization they have to study proposed bills and recommend their adoption or rejection. A committee's decision is considered to be a principal factor in determining a draft law's future. If the committee supports the draft law, the probability of its adoption by the Council is high. It is rare that a draft law opposed by a committee is adopted by the Council. So far, the Council has set up fifteen specialized permanent committees.

Council meetings are plenary sessions of the entire Council. They are normally public, but the Council can meet in camera at the request of the President of the Republic, of the government, of the Council chairman or of a minimum of ten Council members.

The *Shura* Council is to be in permanent session. It routinely meets from the beginning of March till the end of June and from first of September till the end of December. The Council chairman decides upon extra-ordinary meetings. He has to summon the Council if one third of the members or the President of the Republic request it to consider specific matters put on its agenda.

The internal regulations of the Council require it to meet in ordinary sessions each Monday unless the Council decides otherwise. The chairman calls for a meeting by giving prior notice of at least 48 hours. He submits the agenda, memoranda and other drafts, if they have not been distributed previously.

Guarantees for the Shura Council's Independence

For the Council members to fulfill their tasks in complete liberty, it is necessary that certain guarantees should exist protecting members from unlawful influence or intimidation. This in turn safeguards the public interest and enhances the Council's independence. Article 58 of the PC provides that no member of the *Shura* Council can be held accountable for reports or ideas that he may proffer in the Council or its committees or for his voting in public or secret meetings of the

Council. This provision does not apply to any insults or defamation uttered by a member (Article 59). Members of the Council enjoy immunity from investigation, inspection, arrest or imprisonment or any other penalty. Action against a Council member can only be taken with the sanction of the Council unless he is caught red-handed. In this case the Council must be duly informed.

Incompatibilities of Council Membership and other Public Positions

Article 49 of the Constitution provides that a member of the *Shura* Council should not at the same time be a public employee. Moreover, articles 28 and 31 of the Election Law No. 29 of 1980 provide that every public employee who is nominated to the *Shura* Council is expected to resign as soon as his nomination has been confirmed. Undoubtedly, such a prohibition is in fact an affirmation of the Council member's independence as he is then free of the "inducement and intimidation" of his employers, especially those within the government that he is supposed to control.

Parliamentary Remuneration

Although not stated in the Constitution, the Council's internal regulations in Article 121 provide that "members are entitled to remuneration from the date of rendering the constitutional oath".

The prohibition from holding Council membership and a public post simultaneously seeks to preserve the member from falling prey to bribery and misrepresentation. In modern systems it is normal that a specific remuneration or "honorarium" be granted to the parliamentarian to facilitate the performance of his task by guaranteeing his material independence.

Powers of the Shura Council

In its first articles the PC states that "Yemen is an independent and sovereign Islamic Arab state," and that it is "a revolutionary representative republic." Moreover, Article 44 states that the *Shura* Council is the supreme legislature of the state. Article 45 provides that the *Shura* Council undertakes supervision of the acts of the executive. Article 1 of the Council's internal regulations appoints the *Shura* Council as the legislative body that has ultimate powers of legislation and the power of control over the acts of the executive authority.

The Constitution gives the *Shura* Council a "legislative authority". The Council is to approve and enact laws in fundamental and original terms. In addition the Council exercises a specific "political role" by controlling the government in all of its policies and activities as is ordained by Article 4 of the Council's internal regulations. Control over the acts of the executive means responsible positive participation on the part of the legislative body to safeguard the gains of the nation, realize social justice on the basis of Islam through constant evaluation of national progress, bringing into prominence its positive aspects, drawing appropriate lessons to deal with the negative aspects, confront deviations and ensure the executive organs' effectiveness in responding to the vital requirements of building society and a modern state. This in return will further social progress and raise the citizens' standard of living.

Article 5 of the internal regulations clarifies that the relationship between the legislative and executive branches is based on cooperation, full understanding and compatibility. The Council discusses and approves the government's budget, its expenditures and resources. This is its "financial power" in addition to its "founding power" to amend the constitution and its "judicial power" related to the duties of the Supreme Constitutional Court.

The Council pursues its functions as provided for in the PC and the NC fully, like any other representative council in any modern democratic state in the world. It exercises control over the state and its organs through a series of measures beginning with the enactment of legislation pertaining to the establishment and regulation of the Council and the securing of financial means required for its proper functioning and activities. The Council, through its specialized committees, also follows up on the realization of the aims of legislation so as to ensure sound expenditure of public funds. The committees study in detail the annual reports of the various establishments.

The *Shura* Council in the Yemen Arab Republic is a young establishment and its members are beginners in representative work. They can make this Council a great power, providing much needed control over a sound and effective administration. There is also the hope that the Council will fulfill its functions in proper manner and its members will truly be the representatives of the people.

The NC states: "As the *Shura* Council represents the people, the democratic practice of rights and the fulfillment of responsibilities do not emanate from a right inherent in the members themselves. Nor is it a right which members are given by electoral districts. Members are rather exercising rights on behalf of all the people. These are indigenous rights. Representatives are responsible for rendering their duties and bear the consequence of any shortcomings."

1) "AL IMAN" in the forties and "AL NASR" newspaper in the fifties: see also Muhammad Hasan, "The Heart of Yemen".
2) Abdullah Ath-Thawr, "Yemen's Revolution - 1948 - 1968" p. 81
3) Abdullah Adh-Dhayfani, "Nationalistic Traits in the Movement of the Free Yemenis - 1944-1948, unpublished dissertation; University of Cairo
4) Edgar O'Ballance, "The War in Yemen", page 30
5) Harlin Clark, "Unpublished reports to the US State Department"; Clark's reports were presented to me in 1981 while visiting him in his home in Denver, Colorado
6) Mutahhar Muhammad Ismael Al-Izzi, "Constitutional Development in Yemen", p. 27
7) ibidem, p. 271; "Documents of Yemen", published by the Ministry of Information
8) Al-Izzi, p. 272
9) NC, Introduction
10) ibidem, p. 5
11) "Understanding the NC" by the General Secretariat of the Permanent Committee, August 1984
12) ibidem, p. 17
13) Al-Izzi, pp. 471-472
14) "Understanding the NC", p. 18
15) ibidem, p. 18
16) NC, chapter 2
17) PC, article 4
18) NC, Man and his Country
19) See also article 28 of election law No.8 of 1975
20) Article 46 of PC
21) Article 51 of PC
22) See article 71 of PC
23) NC, chapter 2
24) See articles 61 and 107 of PC
25) Article 76 of PC; chapter 2 of NC
26) Article 65 of PC; chapter 2 of NC
27) NC, chapter 1
28) ibidem
29) PC, article 5
30) NC, Introduction
31) NC, chapter 2
32) ibidem
33) PC, article 5
34) NC, chapter 2
35) ibidem
36) PC, article 32
37) NC, chapter 2
38) ibidem
39) ibidem
40) PC, article 42
41) ibidem
42) PC, article 24
43) PC, article 29
44) PC, article 27
45) PC, article 26
46) NC, chapter 2
47) PC, article 28
48) PC, article 25
49) PC, article 39
50) NC, chapter 2
51) PC, article 36
52) PC, article 12
53) PC, article 33

54) NC, chapter 3
55) NC, chapter 2
56) NC, chapter 3
57) ibidem
58) ibidem
59) ibidem

The Cooperative Movement: a Basis for Democratic Development

by Ahmad Muhammad Al-Harbi

Democracy as a concept evolved in various forms as the most appropriate manner of administrating the social environment. The crucial point of this concept lies in the creation of a body of public representatives responsible for the administration of the society's affairs. Success is tied to the extent to which such a body can be renewed. Democracy magnifies the ability of representatives to participate in the decision making process of the government and ensures the implementation of decisions. This necessitates the creation of an institutional setup duly considering plurality within the structure in accordance with the specific balance of all social forces. Thereby the regularity and continuity of the process is ensured.

Cooperative Work in Yemen's History

The type of civilization of any nation is closely related to the type and manner of democracy adopted. Each civilization has its distinctive character and specific characteristics even though some features may be held in common with other civilizations. Age-old characteristics of the Yemeni civilization exist to this day testifying to greatness and durability for more than 5000 years. Yemeni culture has always had its specific traits, especially that of putting achievements to the service of society. The Yemen is an ancient society which constructed dams and the first irrigation systems based on scientific understanding. Links were established between agricultural production and commercial activities. It was a society that directed each citizen towards work and production, giving each and everyone a share in the development of an ancient civilization. All citizens bore the responsibility of maintaining and preserving the civilization on the basis of rules, traditions and decrees determining their individual roles. In this manner it was guaranteed that all enjoyed the fruits of their civilization, such as prosperity, happiness, and dignity on an equal basis. [1]

While man always attempted to secure his livelihood through work, especially agricultural work, the Yemenis were among the first to promote work based on cooperation and democratic principles. Throughout more than 5 millennia, the Yemenis not only established a successful agricultural economy, rightly considered to be one of the oldest in human history, but also sought its expansion through the construction of terraces as a direct response to the increasing population. All this was based upon participation and cooperation. The efforts, energies and potentials of the inhabitants were mobilized and directed towards ensuring a surplus in production. Thus, the people achieved a high level of security, enabling them to lead a peaceful and relaxed life within the confines of rugged mountains. Food requirements were ensured and the land safeguarded for people fully cooperating and supporting each other.

Because of these fortunate conditions, the ancient Yemeni people were able to build a flourishing civilization based on the use of scientific achievements in agriculture, commerce and art within a framework of cooperation. During this period cooperative work became a most powerful tool for increased production and a highly refined organization of the activities of the state and society. Does this mean that cooperative work occupied an advanced position in social life? If so, what factors made it possible to raise it to such an advanced level?

Civilization is an expression of organized and mobilized efforts within society. The totality of such efforts undoubtedly is governed by a central axis, the source of all public actions. This central axis is the connection between work and production. "Ancient Yemeni social groups were composed of segments and sections enjoying equality in economic and social rights. Every clan of each tribe was under the supervision of the tribe. To ensure equal treatment compatible with the position of each clan, the clans and tribes formed one nation that had its own rules thus the link that connected all individuals was a compulsory one and not a voluntary one. Each group or class had to live within the limits defined for it and abide by the directives set by the state. Consequently, the state's economic order was somewhat akin to the form of a pyramid, at whose apex stood the king even though the monarchy was not always an absolute one." [2]

The people making up the tribes, be they ruling tribes or ruled by others, were all concerned and entrusted with responsibilities. The leadership position of the ruling tribes did not exempt them from service for the sake of public welfare. This affirms the fact that the connection between work and production was the axis and basis of all social and economic activities. Within this framework there were no differences between individuals or between tribes. All worked and produced to satisfy needs and increase the wealth of the community according to the rules spelling out concerning relationships between land, work and people.

Work requirements, the nature of the land and political and administrative conditions played an important role in determining the status of a tribe. To avoid being split up into smaller fragments, tribes often united with others, creating a federation. This system aided the development of Yemen's ancient society and the formation of civilized and settled tribes as can be studied in the history of ancient Saba.

Yemeni Cooperative Work - Genesis and Early Achievements

Cooperation is certainly a phenomenon related to human existence since ancient times, but with differing and even disparate practical and behavioral patterns and concepts. It has played an important role during stages of human development, leading from one stage to another. It led to the recognition of the need for social reforms, contributing towards the creation of a higher level of civilization for humanity. History tells us that human beings in their perpetual search for a better life have adopted various types of activities. They never stood idle before the complexities of life and the secrets of nature, patiently awaiting the inevitable, rather, they searched, studied and used all of their competence including intellectual, physical and organizational capabilities to master and develop nature, making and shaping human history and creating a heritage for the sake of a better life and the happiness of all humanity.

Cooperative work which has its origin in ancient Yemeni history, has always been one of the main tools for directing society's agricultural activities to satisfy needs for food, thereby erecting a highly advanced civilization. It linked men to the land and had them wield the sword in defense of it. One of the highly important manifestations of this cooperative concept is that both the sword and a piece of land were the right of each citizen. Thus a Yemeni civilization with a highly elaborate social structure emerged, regulating all efforts to maintain and develop agriculture. Unfortunately these developments did not continue unchallenged. Instead, Yemeni civilization at times deteriorated greatly and agricultural production collapsed as a result of internal dissension and conflict, repeated foreign invasions and the cruel nature of systems that make uneconomic use of nature. This took place especially under the imams, whose rule lasted more than 300 years, causing immense harm and bringing untold hardship to the land and the people.

The totality of domestic and external factors affecting Yemen during the various phases of its history not only led to the neglect of the irrigation systems thus causing agriculture to deteriorate rapidly, but also caused damage to arable land and led to the emergence of agricultural entities that introduced oppression and various forms of subjugation and social dependence.

The social life that appeared under the rule of the imams, lasting for more than 300 years, is characterized by the inhabitants of rural Yemen living in small communities, each community constituting a separate social unit. Their life had not changed much from ancient times and was little different from that of the urban centers. The family remained the primary unit headed by the father and was comprised of children, grandchildren, women and other relatives. Change was only possible when the sons formed independent families after the father had died. Thus, the only manifestation of independence on the part of the sons came with the division of the estate after the father's death.[3]

This country, which is capable of ensuring the food needs of some thirty million persons, as estimated by some experts, witnessed very cruel social, economic, cultural and political conditions. During various periods Yemen suffered famines. The lack of transportation and communication facilities was one of the more prominent features which impeded development. The deteriorating irrigation systems were left without repair. The life of the peasants lacked the most basic element of security. The absence of preventive and curative health services led to the spread of chronic and endemic diseases. Numerous epidemics constituted a serious obstacle to any development. All these conditions were used by the imams to perpetuate their rule until the dawn of the September Revolution of 1962.

The so-called triad of 'disease, ignorance and poverty' was a prominent feature of social, economic and political life in Yemen prior to the 26 September Revolution of 1962; furthermore, the absence of a sound social perception of the means of tackling this triad compounded by mismanagement from the Imamic regime reduced Yemeni society to a state of misery. It was, in fact, a mixture of deteriorating economic conditions and the nature of the regime, possibly derived from clan values and theological ideals, that divided society in two classes: a theocratic class made up of those wielding power before the revolution, including social segments close to the source of power by virtue of their social positions, such as judges and government employees, and the deprived class of workers, peasants and other producers. This latter class was not given a respectable social position owing to the values and concepts that prevailed during those times. Manual labor was not appreciated or given due respect On the contrary, productive work was held in low esteem and those who pursued it were placed at the very bottom of the social scale. Such a view dealt a severe blow to the concept of cooperative work. Cooperative work was no longer desired or directed towards production and placing the achievements of civilization at the service of society. New educational, political and economic concepts and values held sway, and their only aim was the oppression and subjugation of man, killing any aspirations for development for the benefit of society.

Cooperatives as Forms of Social Solidarity

In the face of all these manifestations of oppression and subjugation on the part of the theocratic rule of the imams, society had no chance but to resort to whatever remained of the inherited concept of cooperative work, even if it went against the policy of the imams. The most common and important manifestations of cooperation were the following:

Village Cooperative

This type of activity was based on voluntary work to which the men of a single village would contribute. It was also extended to cover other villages, especially in projects such as public utilities from which all residents of the village or administrative unit would benefit. This type of cooperative work is distinguished by the fact that it combined elements of choice and obligation at the same time. The basic arrangement was that those who did not contribute with manual labor were obliged to contribute with materials or finances. Contributions in kind were either foodstuff, tools or cash.

Village cooperation was not limited to work on public utilities. It was also practiced to overcome natural disasters, save yields from damage and protect the soil from being eroded. One of the more distinct features of this kind of cooperative work was the willingness of the residents to stand side by side brandishing their weapons to counter a foreign threat. The next moment they would pick up their axes and hoes and proceed to other tasks. They would gather in the fields during sowing and harvest time and work together with speed and precision. They would not receive any wages, yet not one would fall behind because the day would inevitably come when the individual would need help.

Cooperation by Affiliation

This second form of cooperation with historic roots was carried out in accordance with the set of rules and patterns inherited from ancient times.[4] It was expressed through affiliation of blood, locality and wealth. Each resident was called upon to participate according to his ability, thus in fact underlining the affiliation to his group. The ability to participate was based on an estimate of the type of holding, its return, the type of ownership and its size, even if this was within the confines of the social unit. As long as the resident was related to the unit by lineage, residence or links, he was considered part of it. The owner or holder was thus enjoined to contribute to the extent of his capability. Nobody could withdraw from such an arrangement without risking expulsion from the social unit. This type of solidarity was also used to ease the unjust treatment imposed by the rulers.

Pasture cooperation

This form of cooperation was linked to farming and animal husbandry which was and still is an important component of economic activity. Pastures are divided among and allocated to groups of residents. Those who herd animals are subject to such division and the regulations accompanying it. The allotted areas were subject to extremely strict disciplinary rules which could not be violated. Thus, a section would be open for grazing for a period and then left fallow. All had to abide with the rules. Any contravention would open the perpetrator to penalties that could well be harsh at times.

Cooperation for Irrigation

In addition to cooperation in herding and sharing pastures, there also was a closely knit cooperation in regulating irrigation. The country does not possess all-year-round rivers and the traditional irrigation system had deteriorated. Irrigation was only possible through springs and wells. This fact necessitated regulation whereby each citizen would have access to quantities of water actually needed for household and farming purposes. Periodic alternation of access to water came into practice which follow rules according proximity to the spring or well. Water was rationed in accordance with the number of individuals in the household and average daily consumption. A similar pattern related to irrigation of cultivable land. When necessary, priority was given to those whose crops were threatened by lack of rain. Newcomers to the unit were also given preferential access.

Other Forms of Cooperation

Besides the aforementioned forms of cooperation there were other forms specifically designed to meet and overcome natural disasters, assist victims of disasters and aid the sick and feeble. All of these forms contributed to the reinforcement of social solidarity among the inhabitants.

Forms of Cooperation and the Employment of Democratic Means

The forms of cooperation society resorted to in order to confront the harsh conditions created by isolation and backwardness imposed by the Imamic regime, in fact, represented a type of non-governmental social organization. The cooperative forms adopted by Yemeni society to direct its own affairs are considered highly important social developments. Voluntary work on a collective basis combined choice and obligation in social and economic activity. There was a fair degree of understanding and sound appreciation of material participation based on the principle of 'from each according to his ability'. None could renounce the responsibility of participating in this effort, be it in form of manual effort or by contributing needed materials, tools or cash. All were subject to participation according to ability and all benefited economically. Furthermore, all were equally subject to a set of disciplinary measures and penalties. The implementation of this set of rules, sometimes written, but often not, was assigned to individuals whose powers reached from the aqil, or head of the village, to the shaykh of the locality, the district and higher levels. The nature of powers and responsibilities of these individuals was determined by previously agreed upon rules pertaining to each type of activity and each form of cooperation. Where, then was democracy to be found? Democracy manifested itself in the following forms:
- A pyramidically shaped distribution of power in the settlement of disputes meant that any dispute among residents of the village had first to be submitted to the village head. If he was able to come up with a solution compatible with customs and traditions and acceptable to all, then the matter would end there. Should there be further objections, it would be referred to the shaykh of the locality and finally to the shaykh of the district whose ruling would be binding upon all.
- The parties involved in any given dispute had the firmly established right to make use of the various arguments that aided their cause. They had the right to make their views known to the other party and to the arbitrator. If a consensus could be reached, the matter would be settled. If not, the dispute

would be subjected to the next higher level of the hierarchy. This is not just a simplified form of litigation. The free expression of views by others concerning particular dispute constituted a form of democratic exercise whereby the minority submitted to the majority. Moreover, these consultations and expressions of views served as a precedent for solving similar disputes in the future.

- Was this structure of power subject to a conscious selection process as an expression of democracy? As a matter of fact, the shaykh was the ultimate authority and was generally not elected by the people however, he was selected because of his social standing, his soundness of mind, his mental and intellectual abilities and other qualities justifying his particular social status. Because of the required education and upbringing, this office was traditionally passed on to the shayk's sons. Other persons who wished to exercise authority, had to prove they possessed the same qualities in order to gain the confidence of the people. Only by proving that they can shoulder responsibilities can they be recognized as deserving their position. Being ignored was a sure sign of rejection by the people. The entire system rested on a set of recognized customs and values that had to be taken into account, even by the central government, which found it impossible to bypass them.
- These cooperative forms amalgamated social acceptance and public desires. They also merged other aspects that constitute the very basis of democracy as the most appropriate form of administering the affairs of society such as the prohibition of evil and the defense of human rights.

The 26 September Revolution of 1962 and the New Structure of Cooperatives

The socioeconomic structures inherited by the 26 September Revolution were weak and, in one way or the other, had an effect on the emergence of new cooperative structures. These previous structures also influenced the forms of new cooperatives. The types of cooperative organizations and the contents of their operation were based on the concept of self-reliance. Meeting the many needs of society was the starting point for their establishment, especially the need for education, health, communication, transport and social welfare as well as the need for food, shelter and clothing. This led to new forms of cooperative work with new characteristics:[5]

The Cooperative Movement

- Yemenis had inherited backwardness and had many diverse needs and so were anxious to meet development objectives by interacting with the revolution and advancing its goals. The people were also keen on unifying the political administration of their society. Citizens took the initiative by establishing diverse projects such as building roads, schools and clinics.
- Realism was a new aspect of cooperative work based on popular initiative. Realism here means linking the aspirations to actual needs within the framework of national capabilities. In other words, realistic perceptions were based on a realistic perception of needs and then translated into projects that satisfied these needs. There was a real need for schools, clinics and roads; however, it was the perception of these needs that determined their priorities combined with a policy of minimizing costs. The construction of a road, for example, constituted the precondition for further cooperative work. The completed road facilitated the transportation of materials, equipment and other utilities required for the construction of schools and clinics and other establishments. Thus a down-to-earth approach was taken in order to satisfy the many needs of the community.
- Work was carried out through private initiative with a sense of truth, pragmatism and administrative routine which made the projects less costly. They were accomplished in record time, overcoming the biggest obstacles.

The most important aspect of this type of cooperative work was the application of democracy with regards to management and determination of objectives. Needs were many and diverse, but initiatives were extensive and widespread, though official resources were limited. Organization and structure were needed to accomplish goals. There was no option other than democracy as an appropriate means for directing the various activities. Democracy was adopted in an irregular manner, by selecting local leaders who channeled the citizen's sentiments and zeal for cooperative work in implementing the decisions taken by consensus. A certain number of representatives were selected from among the people to follow up projects and assist the local leadership. Material support required for projects was made available. Advice was given to improve the work in progress. Difficulties were overcome by clarification of the issues and their social and economic implications for the people concerned.

Certain rules were established such as the principle of civic responsibility for leadership in managing local projects. Everybody had the freedom to remain or withdraw from public positions of responsibility. There was a periodic renewal of voluntary leadership agreed upon during the meetings of the residents and workers in the various projects.

New frameworks of cooperative work were created and structures were developed in subsequent years as cooperatives spread to numerous parts of the various provinces. They soon became social organizations, expressing the residents' needs and aspirations.

Village project committees were created between 1963 and 1965; Local Development Boards between 1965 and 1972; District Development Boards between 1972 and 1974; Local Development Associations between 1975 and 1985; and Local Councils for Cooperative Development from 1985 onward.

Cooperative Democracy in Practice

Historically speaking, democracy has been defined as 'rule of the people by the people'. The history of the development of democracy has been a painful one. The people usually had to face ruling regimes that severely curtailed the rights of the citizens to self expression and free participation in government affairs. Most people were deprived of any rights in the absence of justice, law, and equal rights including the right to legitimate self-defense.

This was also the case in Yemen where a long and arduous struggle had to be waged in order to attain democracy which was finally achieved after the eruption of the 26th September Revolution in 1962. The goals of this struggle were formulated in the National Charter which defined democracy as follows:

> *"Democracy means that the state with its various powers exists for the sake of the people. The people are the source of all authority."*[6]

To make matters clearer the Charter goes on to state:

> *"There can be no sovereignty on the basis of lineage, money, personality cults, religious sects or special group of persons. All citizens form one united social structure that derives its life from each member and provides each with his needs. Life is regulated by constitutional institutions on the basis of cooperation, love and fraternity."*[7]

Cooperative democracy could be considered to be the best form of democracy in both qualitative and quantitative terms. Its original concept can be found in simple social relationships. Freedom for the people becomes necessary in order to allow them to participate in power sharing and to play an effective role in change and progress. The scope of this participation is determined by the level of democracy achieved by the state's administrative apparatus. In practical terms this means that cooperative democracy is closely linked with the level and extent of democracy practiced within society itself as well as in the state apparatus. If such democracy is absent or its scope limited, there will be restraints upon cooperative democracy as well.

Does this mean that the general level of democracy in any society can be considered an indicator for determining the level of cooperative democracy? It has been postulated that the presence of democracy within the administrative apparatus of the state does not necessarily guarantee general democratic practice. Cooperatives can exercise their democratic rights in full liberty only if general democracy is ensured within society. There has to be a working balance between general democracy at one level and cooperative democracy at a second level which directly benefits from the support and backing provided by democracy in general.

The Yemeni cooperative experience brings into prominence yet another facet of democratic practice. The cooperative movement produced organizational frameworks at the levels of the project, the village and the administrative unit. Institutions developed respectively through village committees, then development boards and finally development councils. It is the development of democratic practice which pressured the administrative apparatus to give official recognition.

On the other hand, some of the more problematic aspects of the Yemeni cooperative experience should also be noted here. It is a fact that despite well established norms for the management of cooperatives, there always has been a profound and deep influence exerted by certain individuals on the way cooperatives were run. Critics have even claimed that the whole cooperative democratic experience has failed and should be discarded altogether.

Yet this manifestation is really an exception to the rule. It is a fact that it was the people who were behind the establishment of the cooperative movement. They exhibited talent at mobilizing and organizing which gave great impetus to the movement. The people also exhibited a high degree of control over the affairs of their cooperatives thus it is not true that cooperatives lacked democratic features and were subject to the direction and domination of individuals. Even if there were exceptions to the rule, the fact remains that cooperatives were in general of a democratic and popular nature.

Through democracy it has been possible for cooperatives to develop and strengthen organizationally. This development has led to the emergence of the Local Councils for Cooperative Development formed on the basis of voluntary membership and representation according to the free choice of members of the cooperatives living in a given village or region. The Councils are now able not only to organize their own funds but also to obtain other financial resources to execute development projects benefiting all residents in the region. They remain free of the fetters imposed by administrative routine and are subject only to the collective control exercised by the members.

One of the interesting aspects of the development of the cooperative movement has been its successful resistance to attempts by the administrative apparatus to limit the effectiveness of the movement. It is a fact that the cooperatives did succeed in realizing numerous important projects in the fields of communication, education and health. This success in itself produced new demands, specifically demands for technical expertise to ensure the operation and maintenance of projects. These demands could not be met by the residents alone and pressure was put upon the administrative apparatus of the government to increase support. It was only natural that these requests should be met with resistance. Indeed the administrative structure of the government in turn sought to limit the influence of the cooperatives which of course created conflict because the democratic nature of the cooperatives was based on popular participation and emerged from the desire of the citizens to satisfy basic needs. In order to protect themselves, cooperatives were able to come up with new forms of self-defense. Among these new forms of an institutional nature was the founding of the Local Development Associations which by 1972 numbered 27. This was followed by preparations to convene a general congress resulting in the founding of the first democratic cooperative institution in the country in June 1973 in the form of the Confederation of Yemeni Development Associations (CYDA). This confederation coordinated the efforts of the cooperative associations. It supported programs set up by each association to fulfill the needs of citizens in accordance with available resources.

A new form of cooperative funding of projects emerged in the form of a tripartite funding scheme. The total cost of every project undertaken by each association was split into three equal parts: the LDA itself would raise one third of the cost from residents. By collecting the zakat, the residents themselves would provide the second third and the state would provide the final third of the cost of the project as a subsidy to local development.

From 1973 till 1981 the number of LDA's increased from 14 to 200, all based on the provisions of Law No. 35 of 1975. The LDAs received the status of incorporate bodies administered by managing boards consisting of 7 to 9 persons. The board was to be elected through free, direct and secret ballot by the members of the General Assembly chosen from among the residents on the basis of one representative for every 500 residents. Those receiving the highest number of votes would occupy leading positions on the boards, such as the position of president, general secretary and financial secretary.[8]

Within ten years the LDAs held five General Congresses that dealt with numerous issues related to their activities in local development. The administrative board of the Confederation is made up of representatives of the various governorates taking responsibility for the overall coordination of the various activities of the LDAs throughout the Republic. The administrative board was elected by the General Congress. The membership also included representatives of the service related ministries. Finally, each governorate had its own council of coordination.

Numerous important accomplishments were realized, such as the construction of roads, schools, clinics, health centers, the provision of potable water and electricity, the building of mosques, the establishment of parks and various other projects. The following table gives an impression of the various projects executed through the LDAs in various parts of the Republic and is a living testimony to the effectiveness of cooperative work in the development process.[9]

Area	Project	Volume during 1973-1984
transportation	mountain roads	33,713 kilometers
education	classes	10,524 classes
health	clinics	769 units
water	complete projects	4,244 projects
other areas	parks, etc.	769 projects

The overall cost for implementing these projects during the period 1973 - 1984 amounted to YR 1,840,885,000 (one billion 840 million). Part of it came in the form of in-kind contributions.

Local Development Associations and the Development of Cooperative Democracy

Numerous attempts were made to evaluate the cooperative experience up to the end of 1984. On the basis of the intellectual and theoretical fundamentals of the National Charter, it has been possible to evaluate the cooperative experience and come up with certain conclusions and recommendations necessary for the continuity of the experiment. The development of administrative and organizational concepts and structure is necessary. There is also a need to expand the base of popular participation.

The promulgation of Law No. 12 of 1985 concerning the establishment of the Local Councils for Cooperative Development (LCCD) effectively dealt with these issues. The LCCD's were empowered to propose, administer and operate projects and public utilities in accordance with the rules and regulations in force at the level of each administrative unit.[10]

The LCCD's are considered incorporate bodies enjoying financial and administrative independence and are empowered to administer projects on the level of their respective administrative units. Law No. 12 of 1985 furthermore laid down a more advanced system of democratic practice. Popular representation was to be effected through general elections to the Local Councils. Elections were to be governed by Elections Law No. 79 of 1980 stipulating a free, direct and secret ballot in accordance with a set of qualifications and requirements to be fulfilled by the candidates. Every 500 residents elected one representative into the general assemblies of the LCCD's.

On the basis of the last population census, the country was divided into more than 1,750 electoral units. Candidates were nominated for election into the general assemblies of the LCCD's, as well as membership in the sub-congresses of the People's General Congress on the provincial and district levels.

More than 25,000 citizens competed in these elections. 17,509 eventually became members in the general assemblies of the 209 LCCD's in 209 administrative units. With this election the cooperative movement began to enter a new phase. This is true especially regarding the following points:

1. the identification of financial sources for funding local development activities based on the results of field studies which determine the type and magnitude of primary and essential needs of citizens;
2. an increase in the effectiveness of popular participation and an improved ability to plan, fund, execute, follow-up and evaluate the work of the LCCD's in each administrative unit;
3. the creation of administrative structures within the LCCD's based on the studies of the General Assembly as the supreme authority for supervision and control; the overall technical, administrative and financial supervision of the LCCD's was given to the General Secretariat, which is composed of the following members:
    a) the Higher Administrative Board of the Secretariat consisting of elected and appointed officials; the elected members come from the sub-congresses of the LCCD's in each governorate and are elected for a three year term; the appointed members and representatives of the service-related ministries that are directly associated with the activities of the LCCD's as specified in Law No. 12 of 1985;
    b) the General Secretariat's Executive Office is made up of nine general departments, headed by members of the Administrative Board and are run by a technical expert in each specific area;
    c) the branch secretariats of the General Secretariat's Executive Office are headed by the Minister of State according to the provision of the law; they are administered in each governorate by an elected member and by a general director specialized in the activities to be undertaken by the branch secretariat.

Democracy in the Daily Operations of the Cooperatives

Democracy in practice rests upon certain democratic principles which are beyond contention. Among the most important proofs of democracy being practiced in the cooperatives are the following:
1. A flexible and open policy is being propagated based on general democratic principles accepted by the great majority of the residents. The application of this policy has made cooperative democracy able to face certain challenges in society by employing appropriate methods to reinforce the general democratic course of society.
2. The leadership continues to rely upon a popular base through purposeful dialogue which increases objectivity. Serious efforts are being undertaken to deepen links between the leadership and the people through on-going contacts, field visits and meetings to ascertain people's views. Correct information is being transmitted to the quarters responsible for directing public affairs.
3. People are guaranteed adequate participation in various issues of political decision making affecting their lives. This also includes the dissemination of information to the people to ensure their effective participation in the development process. This is also to ensure that the individuals in each administrative unit actually exercise their rights of control and supervision. All of this is designed to underline the fact that there is a cooperative sector whose performance is governed by democratic practice, collective view and public participation in planning. It also underlines the responsibility of the citizen to supervise and control the managing bodies of the elected councils.
In this context, the General Secretariat of the LCCD's and its Executive Office regulate cooperative actions. Finances are directed to crucial projects required by the residents. These projects will then have a positive influence upon the lives of local citizens. All citizens are called upon to fulfill the tasks assigned to them, thus ensuring their participation in the concept of collective management.
4. Self-initiative of citizens is to be encouraged thereby deepening creative interaction among them. Support shall be given on the moral, political and material levels, then the citizens will be able to perform their tasks with enthusiasm and undertake fruitful activities in the service of society.
5. The best possible conditions should be created for the best application of democracy leading to more effective popular control over all that is being done in the service of development. This has to be in accordance with the social assignment given to the cooperative movement by the government, so as to fully and continuously satisfy the needs of the people.[11]

As such, the LCCD's had to concentrate their efforts on planning which is the very essence of democratic practice in the process of development. Efforts by cooperatives during the period 1985 - 1988 in the form of funding and implementing projects were indeed successful. The results can be summarized in the following lines:

The Administrative Aspect

The concept of the cooperative administration of a democratic pattern is well developed and has been reflected in a number of measures ensuring lively interaction between the administration and the supervising and controlling organs. Cooperative administration is now following a pattern that ensures collectivity while holding each unit responsible for the cost, the type of accomplishment and the number of citizens benefiting from each project.

The Legal Aspect

For the sake of achieving a certain level of control and continuity in implementing projects and for the sake of effective coordination between the various popular and official activities, the need for legalization arose. Each organization has to fulfill its various responsibilities in accordance with legislation. This prevents any infringement upon fundamental principles and ensures a more disciplined development on the levels of the LCCD's and the government.

The Funding Aspect

The concept of popular participation has been expanded to encompass not only the free expression of opinions and views but also participation in planning, funding, evaluation and follow-up of implementation. It has been underlined that each citizen who happens to be a member of the local council and the sub-congress of the People's General Congress in his region is responsible for each and every administrative act related to any project. In this context the LCCD's have executed a number of projects directly related to the needs of citizens in 1985/1986. The most important ones are:[12]

Area	Volume	Cost
rural roads	852 km	YR 7,648,872
road maintenance	3,836 km	YR 22,449,588
rural schools	783 classes	YR 85,502,293
school maintenance	1,125 classes	YR 12,349,183
potable water	267 projects	YR 60,155,051
potable water (maint.)	66 projects	YR 3,814,689
clinics	71 rooms	YR 6,475,525
clinics (maintenance)	148 rooms	YR 959,356
parks, mosques, etc.	261 projects	YR 45,029,998
maintenance	141 projects	YR 6,105,790
Total expenditure		**YR 270,490,345**

The LCCD's have in total executed 1413 projects at a cost of YR 224,811,739 and carried out maintenance work on 1348 projects at a cost of YR 45,678,606 adding up to a total of YR 270,490,345. At the same time, popular participation in material terms amounted to YR 50,386,991. This contrasts to the drop in popular participation that was felt some years ago.

Historic Significance of Democracy within the Cooperative Movement and its Development within the Framework of the Local Councils for Cooperative Development

The historic significance of democracy practiced in our country within the cooperative movement lies in the fact that we have never considered democracy to be a marginal phenomenon. It is rather the embodiment of cultural, social, economic and political structures rooted in the ancient, medieval and modern history of Yemen. Development of democracy is consistent with our country's social, economic and political history. Some may attempt to minimize the role of democracy by relegating it to specific historic periods. Citizenship may be a fundamental human right defining a person's relation to a homeland, but it is citizenship which also places certain obligations upon the citizen towards his society and homeland. Citizenship is meaningless without having the citizen fulfill these obligations.

The cooperative experience has underlined the truth of such a relationship. It has also underlined the fact that the rights the citizen include participation in planning, implementation, funding, follow-up and evaluation of the various processes taking place within a specific administrative unit and geographical area.

The basic concept of general democracy recognizes the right of the citizen to choose his representative to the various cooperative organizations. It also recognizes his right to exercise supervision and control over the work of elected bodies. This enables democracy to occupy a place at the heart of the society and become the motor for social and economic development.

If cooperative democracy, within the context of a general democracy, has proven that it is neither a slogan nor a mere statement, then society cannot do without democratic institutions. Such institutions are not mere elected local councils, rather they are the instrument through which the individual can make use of his right to express his views and participate in public work within the framework of a legal organization. The free exercise of rights ensures the continuation of development, eventually leading towards a better life. Democracy itself needs to develop as a live organization rather than a mechanical and unreflected copy of certain models. Then it will lead to the establishment of social justice in place of exploitation. It is also destined to expand its base rather than narrowing it. Consolidation of democracy is the sure means of confronting political oppression, realizing unity and proceeding ahead discarding dissent and division.

Within the context of general democracy the LCCD's seek to realize a number of democratic functions. The most important ones are the following:

- One goal is to establish a clear and widespread awareness of cooperative ideas within society. This in itself is a measure for success and creates the right conditions for a further expansion of cooperation and participation.
- Another aim is to expand the base of popular participation by consolidating the democratic conduct of management and planning in local development. This has been affirmed by the laws regulating the operation of the LCCD's. This in turn has led to the protection of the numerous rights of the citizen, enabling him to pursue his activities and to shoulder his responsibilities.
- The LCCD's prepare social, economic and cultural programs that encourage such behavior aiding social and economic development of the various regions and directing all local resources to the local councils enabling them to fulfill their purpose.
- There is a general tendency by the General Secretariat, its Executive Office and its branches in the governorates to permeate social and economic organizations with cooperative and democratic ideas. This will ensure the continuity of cooperative activities and lead to improved working methods.
- The LCCD's aim to protect the fundamental democratic rules adopted by the local councils. The most important among these rules is equality among all members in terms of rights and obligations. Mutual assistance remains the basis of work for the public interest and underlines collectivity and loyalty to the principles of cooperation.

The Cooperative Movement

- The LCCD's insist on subjecting the results of all activities to evaluation. Cooperative activities must not be mere abstracts. They must be tangible results whose positive effects upon the population must be known and felt.
- It is important to consolidate the various educational aspects so as to increase the awareness of the citizens. Cooperative activities must be directed towards vocational specialization, the deepening of political awareness, strengthening labor ethics and raising the level of production. This is to be the social and economic function of the LCCD's and has been underlined by the General Secretariat.
- The LCCD's help to overcome problems affecting development, such as wasting social potential and resources. Efforts need to be directed towards improving social security and living standards. Stability can be achieved by work programs, satisfying essential needs and expanding the number of those benefiting from increased production.
- There has been an effort to solve fundamental issues of the national economy by encouraging cooperation in agriculture, especially in producing vegetables and animal fodder. Transforming industries need to be established. The drafting of economic plans needs to be aided through the existing cooperative organizations and institutions.

---

1) see: "The National Charter", Introduction
2) "Political History of the Yemen", Muhammad Yahya Al-Haddad
3) "Considerations of Development in Yemen before the Revolution", Muhammad Anam Ghalib
4) "The Cooperatives and Characteristics of the Yemeni Cooperative Movement, Ahmad Muhammad Al-Harbi
5) "The Yemeni Cooperative Movement, from the First Ideas of Establishment to the Most Recent Developments", Confederation of LCCD's
6) "The National Charter", People's General Congress
7) ibidem
8) "Cooperative Legislation, Part I", Confederation of LCCD's
9) "25 Years of Cooperation", the Local Councils for Cooperative Development
10) Law No. 12 for Local Councils of 1985
11) "The Unfolding of the Cooperative Experience in Practice", lecture by the Secretary General of the LCCD's, 1986
12) "Report of the Secretary General to the Second General Congress of the Local Councils", General Secretariat of the LCCD's, 1988

Winds of Democracy Blowing over Arab Soil

by Sa'd Eddin Ibrahim

For a number of years, or to be more exact, since autumn 1983, a hundred Arab thinkers wanted to meet in order to discuss the topic "the crisis of democracy in the Arab World". At that time they could not find a single Arab capital that would allow them to hold such a meeting. They were thus forced to search for a place outside of the Arab World to be host to their meeting. A few days was considered sufficient time for discussing the problem of democracy openly. The island of Cyprus was chosen as their temporary refuge and there they discussed the issue among other issues relating to the Arab World.

During the last week of March 1989 some 200 Arab thinkers, politicians and unionists met in the Arabian capital Amman to discuss the same topics. This time it was a big conference organized by the Arab Thought Forum.

Between Autumn in Cyprus and Spring in Amman

Approximately 600 km of earth and sea lie between the non-Arabic island of Cyprus and the Arabic capital Amman. The two seminars were divided by approximately 6 years. One of the seminars was in autumn and the other one in spring. The distance between the two places is not a lot and the time lapse between the two events not so great, but what a difference between the two places, the two time periods and the two seasons! The most important difference lay in the atmosphere, just like the difference in air between autumn and spring.

The atmosphere that prevailed during the seminar of the Arab thinkers in Cyprus six years earlier was heavy, sad and downcast. The seminar in Cyprus came after a full year of Israeli assaults upon Lebanon, the siege of Beirut and the expulsion of the Palestinian Liberation Organization. That was followed by the occupation of the city itself. Even more depressing were the massacres at Sabra and Shatila which happened in the autumn of 1982. Throughout the year following these tragic events, Arab thinkers and academics would only meet in small congregations to exchange their views about issues and bewail the misfortune of the Arab World. Some of them later proposed to organize a bigger meeting at an unnamed location in order to exchange views on what should be undertaken to save the Arab Nation from these tragedies. There was a kind of consensus, even before meeting in such a conference that the secret for resolving these problems lies in democracy and in respecting the human rights of the Arab. When they finally decided to go ahead with this meeting, they were looking for an Arab capital in which to meet, but all Arab capitals closed their doors to this opportunity; therefore they were forced to go to Cyprus as was mentioned earlier.

Inspite of the downcast atmosphere that prevailed in the seminar in Cyprus, the participants were determined not to be defeated by this bleak reality. They were determined not to strike their cheeks in despair, tear their clothes and indulge in self-flagellation. A series of other meetings were subsequently held in Cyprus resulting in the foundation of a number of Arab non-governmental institutions aiming at changing the backward Arabic situation through peaceful, industrious and organized activities. Among those new organizations whose seed was planted in Cyprus are:

- the Arab Organization for Human Rights
- the Arab Confederation for Social Sciences
- the Arab Confederation for Political Sciences
- the Arab Confederation for Economic Studies
- the Arab Confederation for Philosophy.

The intention of these new non-governmental Arab organizations was to provide a framework for Arab thinkers and their various specialization. They were meant to be a forum where these thinkers could meet and combine their efforts for the sake of serving the interests of the Arab nation. First and foremost among these issues was to be the issue of democracy and human rights. Soon older Arab organizations aligned themselves with this new movement, including the Union of Arab Lawyers, the Center for Studies on Arabic Unity and the Arab Thought Forum.

These non-governmental Arabic organizations conducted their studies and propagated their work for the sake of democracy and human freedom in the Arab world with great enthusiasm. During the years after the meeting in Cyprus the fruits of their efforts were negligible, yet the patience and persistence of these organizations was not in vain. Beginning in 1985, one would note positive results. Talk about democracy, human freedom and human rights became popular in many circles. Even the ruling Arabic regimes who initially considered such ideas and thoughts an anathema began to entertain new ideas reluctantly.

A much larger number of Arab thinkers, politicians and trade unionists met in

Amman in the spring of 1989 in order to discuss the topic of "political diversity in the Arab World". Before starting they analyzed the situation of the Arab World from 1988 to the present. This time, the conference took place in an Arab capital and there was a great degree of freedom. This was possible on the basis of Arab successes accumulated over the previous two years or, strictly speaking, since the summit meeting in Amman (in November 1987) and the brave Palestinian uprisings (starting December 1987).

Winds of Democracy in Arabia

During the years following the meeting of Arab thinkers in Cyprus, breezes of democracy began to blow gently in the Arab World, affecting one nation after another. Democracy in Egypt which was blocked during the latter period of the late President Anwar Sadat, was revived in the age of President Husni Mubarak. Similar developments happened in Morocco, and beginning in 1985, Sudan also witnessed the removal of one-man-rule by President Ja'far Numayri and the return of democracy in 1986. In 1987, another despotic government ended in Tunis which had held the reins of power in the name of one party, namely the New Constitutional Party. Tunisia changed to a multi-party system. Also the Yemen Arab Republic had its first democratic election in history. In 1988 Algeria witnessed changes leading towards diversification and democracy. Two popular inquiries were held in order to lay the foundation for this change, one to elect the President, and the second for a new constitution allowing a multi-party system for the first time since Algeria's independence in 1962. The year 1988 had not come to an end, when Iraq in the person of President Saddam Hussein announced its determination to change towards democracy. During the first week of April 1989, Iraq witnessed the first democratic parliamentary elections on the basis of a multi-party system. Candidates did not just come from the ruling party, the Socialist Arab Ba'th Party, which had been ruling the country single-handedly since 1968, but also from other parties. In fact, the majority of the candidates for the Iraqi parliament were not from the Ba'th Party.

In conclusion, the breezes of democracy which blew gently and hesitantly during the first half of the 1980s, increased in velocity and by the end of the decade became strong winds. During the 6 years following the meeting of Arab thinkers in Cyprus which was held to promote democracy in the great Arab Nation, democracy took roots in Egypt and Morocco. Democratic changes also began to appear in Sudan, Tunisia, Yemen, Algeria and Iraq. These seven Arab countries comprise some two thirds of the entire Arab world in terms of population. There are two other Arab countries which are candidates for democratic change in the foreseeable future. These are Kuwait and Jordan both of which have experienced a temporary setback due to regional circumstances. Both countries have a long-standing heritage in the practice of democracy. There is no doubt that the winds of democracy will reach a number of other Arab countries as well within the current year or in the 1990's. The 1990's will not come to an end without all Arab nations in one way or the other having accepted democracy.

The Problem of Despotism and Problems of Democracy

Democracy, whose winds have been blowing over Arabian soil during these past years, is also blowing in many other countries of the Third World from the Philippines to Argentina and from Taiwan to Pakistan. Even Eastern Block countries such as the Soviet Union have been exposed to the winds of democracy. Hungary and Czechoslovakia recently underwent decisive changes in the direction of a pluralistic system. Poland has witnessed a fierce struggle with the same objectives, spearheaded by the independent Solidarity Trade Union against the monopoly on power held by the Polish Communist Party. The Solidarity Trade Union achieved great progress throughout the past five years. The same winds of democracy have blown in China and it became obvious to any observer that the battle for democracy in this huge and ancient country has indeed begun. The fights, the bloody events that took place on the Square of Heavenly Peace during the first days of June 1989 only heralded the final countdown for the defeat and end of the one party system in China.

The winds of democracy are inevitably blowing into the countries which are still ruled by a one party system, by a single organization or a single ruler. Powers concentrated in one hand are being dismantled country by country. There are many reasons which cannot be discussed in full detail here. It is sufficient to say that the problems of contemporary societies in the east and the west, in the north and the south, became so complicated and interconnected that one party, one organization or one leader alone finds it impossible to cope with it no matter how successful this party or the ruling establishment or the ruling figure may be, and how much of a genius and whatever broad public base he may claim in his country. Even the "working class" in whose name some one-party systems ruled is no longer ready to accept this form of manipulation. We saw this clearly in Poland. The Polish Communist Party has called itself the representative of the Polish working class since the end of the Second World War; this means that it has ruled more than 40 years; however, the revolution of the Polish working class against the party and the division from the party and the founding of an independent new trade union, the Solidarity Trade Union, clearly shows the displeasure the Polish working class harbored against the hegemony of a one-party system ruling in its name.

The modern working class in today's society is much better educated, much more diversified and has a higher degree of self-consciousness. This class no longer matches with the characteristics of the working class of the 19th Century during the beginning of the "First Industrial Revolution" when Karl Marx in his writings demanded the dictatorship of the proletariat. Since that time the world passed through the "Second Industrial Revolution" during the middle of the 20th Century and the world is now in the last decades of the 20th Century entering the "Third Industrial Revolution". The workers of today are no longer the workers of the past or even the workers of 40 years ago. The workers of today no longer work for 16 hours under harsh circumstances on machines that are operated by coal and steam, as was the case until not so long ago. The workers of today do their work under much more favorable conditions and have acquired a much higher level of self-esteem. Indeed, today's workers are very different. A great variety of differences and even contradictions came up within their own ranks. Some of them began to acquire shares in their own companies, real estate, saving accounts and cars. They became workers and owners simultaneously and in a sense became capitalists; therefore, the polarization between workers and employers is no longer at the same level as it used to be.

In Third World countries, including the Arab World, the one-ruler system became a dilemma, if not a continuous crisis. The sociological map of most of these countries has changed completely since independence in a time frame that spans over the past three decades. A large middle class came into existence together with a modern working class in proportion to the increase in population. The size of the cities doubled. The self-consciousness of the minorities increased together with their demands. Considering the great variety of people in the Arab World, it is impossible for one party or one leader to represent all interests at once and at the same time. To make things even worse, debts and various shortcomings in these societies have been doubling, further demonstrating the inability of one party or one ruler to control these problems; therefore during the past 10 years the societies of the Third World have witnessed widespread public upheavals, especially in the larger cities, tearing apart some of the one-party systems and deposing some of the despotic rulers. Some of these systems have been adaptable enough to submit themselves to a process of democratization and to accept power sharing with others.

The problems of despotism, meaning the rule of one party or one leader, are only too many to enumerate. On the other hand, it does not follow that change towards democracy and pluralism is without any problems. It also does not mean that democracy in itself is able to solve the problems of poverty, debts, backwardness and unjust distribution like a miracle. All democracy means is the releasing of social energies and powers that will enable the society itself, and not through one party or one leader, to face these problems. Democracy is a widely set frame for administering the social concerns in a peaceful way. It is also an excellent method to screen for the best and most competent people to work in the social and national administration. It is a just tool for control and observation in government, increasing the public good and removing harm in government.

At the beginning of each step towards democratic change, and until democracy is firmly established and its values well understood and respected, there will be irresponsible activities and probably tumult and clamor. There will be attempts to forge elections, to manipulate people and sometimes decision making will be extremely slow. These are all phenomena that will of necessity occur and which public opinion must be aware. It is through a well informed public that these negative effects can be overcome. A thousand problems that are the result of democracy are still better than the despotic rule of one man even for one day.

Part II

Electoral Systems and the Future of Democracy in the Republic of Yemen

Selected papers of a two-day seminar sponsored by the
People's General Congress / Sanaa University Branch,
February 16-17, 1992 in Sanaa

The Basic Principles of Election Laws

by Dr. Ahmad Abdurahman Sharafuddin

All contemporary constitutions are concerned with incorporating and highlighting the basic principles of free and democratic elections by describing in detail how these principles work. In the constitution of the Republic of Yemen, these basic principles are well elaborated. Article 41, for example, reads: "The House of Representatives consists of members elected by direct and equitable secret ballot." From the constitutional text, five basic principles emerge relating to the issue of elections:
- Privacy
- Universal Suffrage
- Freedom
- Personal Representation
- Equal Participation

The Principle of Privacy

Privacy aims at guaranteeing the voter's right to cast his vote and electing his representative in complete freedom. No influences or pressures, be they of a material or psychological nature, may be exerted by candidates or individuals supervising the elections.

Here are a couple of points that shed more light on this principle:
- Direct physical pressure may result from the actual presence of armed men in the polling stations and/or from allowing candidates to accompany voters to the ballot box.
- Psychological pressure can be manifested in two ways: tempting voters with promises of financial rewards, and/or intimidating them with threats of revenge and retribution.
- Financial pressures may arise from the candidate's power and ability to purchase voters. This is done by simply distributing money to voters and well known citizens in local constituencies. The exclusive use of mass media by one political power and its candidates, publicizing only its political view and programs is another common violation of election principles. These types of

malpractice are employed by political forces already in power because it is they who have access to the country's resources and money. Also, the mass media are typically under the exclusive jurisdiction of the ruling power which uses them fully for its election campaigns.
- Psychological pressures come in the form of tactical maneuvers practiced by the ruling powers before and during elections. They can greatly influence public opinion by implying that only they favor popular tendencies. Also, popular individuals loyal to the regime may receive much public exposure, encouraging others to follow their examples.

In order to avoid malpractice as described above the law should include the following regulations:
- Within the polling stations, ballot boxes must be placed in a well enclosed area where admission is allowed to voters only.
- The presence of armed soldiers or unauthorized citizens in electoral centers is to be prohibited; security should be maintained from outside the electoral sites only.
- During the period of electoral campaigning, the use of government media should be granted to all parties on an equal basis.
- The use of public funds by the ruling parties needs to be strictly controlled to ensure they are not exclusively used to finance their own election campaigns. Financial regulations should be established that permit all parties equal access to public funds.
- A suitable code of penalties must be established to settle cases of threat, coercion, and other unlawful actions.

The Principle of Universal Suffrage

The principle of universal suffrage aims at guaranteeing the election rights of all citizens, regardless of their education, wealth or social standing. Article 42 of the constitution of the Republic of Yemen emphasizes this principle by putting forward two conditions for voting:
- the voter must be a Yemeni national;
- he must be above 18 years of age.

The article stipulates that people under the eligible age are deprived of the right to elect. Insane people, convicted prisoners and persons who committed crimes of honor or crimes threatening public security are also barred from participating in elections.

· Since the majority of voters are illiterate, the election legislation should adopt the use of special election forms (pictorial forms) to ensure that the illiterate can vote freely, privately and independently. Colors and drawings can be used symbolizing the various candidates. By simply putting his mark besides a pictogram symbolizing a certain candidate, the voter can express his opinion, even through he might be illiterate.

The Principle of Free Elections

This principle guarantees the citizen's freedom to practice his electoral right independent from any outside influence. This principle also includes the freedom of the voter to participate in the election process or abstain from it altogether. Here, the question arises if elections are to be considered the right or the duty of the voter. If it is a right, then the voter has the choice to participate or abstain. If it is defined as a duty, the voter must participate, otherwise he will be liable to prosecution. Countries all over the world differ on this point, either regarding elections as an optional right or a compulsory duty. And if elections are indeed defined as compulsory duty, then the penalty in case of abstaining becomes a further point of discussion. Let it be said that even though compulsory voting may be found useful (because a greater number of voters will go to the polls for fear of punishment), a higher number of voters is only of limited use and the results may even be misleading. The unconvinced voter, motivated by mere fear of penalty, has other ways of expressing his dissatisfaction. He may perhaps knowingly vote contrary to his convictions, leave the electoral card blank, or write nonsense or even critical remarks on his ballot. In such cases, the validity of the electoral card will be nullified, thus there is no sure method for mobilizing a high number of voters.

The Principle of Personal Representation

This principle states that the voter will have to vote personally in his specified constituency. He cannot appoint a representative to vote in his place. The identification of citizens eligible to vote is usually carried out by the supervising committee before the actual balloting.

At election time many voters are not present in their own constituencies where they are registered voters. They may have traveled for such reasons as work, business, etc. In some countries this problem is solved by allowing the voter to nominate a personal representative in the same constituency to vote on his behalf, but this solution has two drawbacks. First, the privacy of the voter is violated once the representative is being told whom to vote for and second, one can never be sure that the representative will actually follow the voter's suggestion.

In our country this problem is limited to just a few groups of people, such as civilian and military employees who are transferred to other places outside their original constituencies, immigrants living abroad, and the supervisory committees during the election process. It must be pointed out though that these three groups consist of a large number of citizens and their constitutional right to vote must be preserved. It is possible that their vote might have a significant impact upon the actual results of the election process. Special laws should be prepared to tackle these problems. Electoral centers can be established in our embassies abroad and specialized electoral committees should deal with the registration and voting process to settle the problems of immigrants and travelers abroad.

Every citizen, whether employed during the election process or not and including the members of the supervisory committees, should be allowed to vote, even if he serves in a constituency which is not his own. The constituency receiving his vote can notify the voter's original constituency in order to register his name. This will ensure that his vote is only counted once.

The Principle of Equal Participation

This principle guarantees equality among all participants in the election process. The constitution reinforces this principle by mentioning the two conditions which must be met in order to vote: to be Yemeni citizen and be over 18 years of age. Any Yemeni who meets these two requirements is eligible and has the right to vote regardless if he is a male or a female member of society.

In addition to the previous five constitutional principles, there is another principle concerning the authenticity of the election process. It refers to an election process that guarantees absolute objectivity, preventing cases of forgery and fraud. Fraudulent handling of ballot boxes, for example, may lead to distorted election results.

There are other measures to be taken in order to safeguard the validity of the election process. One of such concerns is the type of the balloting box. It may be preferred to have the balloting box made of glass, making the contents visible to everybody. The right way of covering and sealing the box is of great importance after the ballots have been cast. This holds equally true for the way a ballot box is opened in order to count votes. In Yemen it is without question that the supervising committee that counts votes is an independent group of people who are in turn observed by members of the various competing parties or their candidates or representatives. The entire election process should always be submitted to strict observation by the judiciary. Ways to appeal against alleged injustice or election fraud should be clarified before the beginning of the election process.

Algeria's Election Experiment

by Ilham Muhammad Mane'

The democratic experiment in Algeria and its political repercussions are widely considered one of the most important political events of our time. Developments in this country received world-wide attention by the newsmedia. Reactions were manifold and from all corners of the world, yet we have to ask ourselves why this experiment should be discussed in a seminar dealing with election laws in Yemen. The reason for doing has two facets:
- Algeria is an Islamic, Arabic and developing country. Political developments in this country are of great concern to all the peoples living in this region and the Arab world.
- The democratic experiment in Algeria does have parallels to the political events in Yemen and is therefore relevant to our country.

Many political analysts consider Algeria as a possible scenario for Yemen, especially in the absence of a genuine democratic process, as far as elections are concerned. It is the free ballot which leads the way to constructive results. The political analysts arguing along this line are correct except for the differences in the political environment and the historical heritage of both countries. On the other hand, there are enough common factors that justify a comparison between the two countries:
- both are going through the experience of a newly born democracy;
- both are suffering from economic problems which affect the life of their citizens;
- multiple political blocks and divergent views affect the political decision making process in both countries.

The following research is divided into an introduction followed by three major parts. The introduction provides an abstract on various concepts of democracy. The first part describes the development of Algeria from a one party system to a multi party system. The second part deals with political reforms and election laws. The third part describes the election of December 26, 1991 and analyses its results.

Concepts of Democracy

Democracy in its literal meaning implies that people rule themselves based on equal rights for all individuals. In reality, however, it is difficult to implement this idealistic view, especially because of the complexities of the state institutions and their multiple tasks. Parliamentary democracy has thus taken three characteristics:
- separation between the three powers (legislative, judiciary and executive)
- parliamentary representation of existing political blocks within an elected parliament
- a multi-party system that assures the peaceful transfer of power from one political party to the other.

The concept of democracy is connected with the idea of the free pursuit of social and economic activities, which in turn guarantees its continuation. There is a clear connection between the social and economic development of the nation and the depth of democratic traditions in its institutions. This does not mean democracy is a product of economic and political development. "When the average income, the level of industrialization, organization and education is high, countries are usually more democratic. Only in a relative prosperous country with a fair distribution of wealth can people enjoy freedom, self-confidence and self-discipline which gives them time and opportunity to participate in building a democratic state. On the other hand, societies divided into a poor majority and a privileged minority always tend to develop some form of oligarchy or outright tyranny."[1]

From a One-Party to a Multi-Party System

The multi-party system in Algeria can be compared with democratic developments in other developing countries even though Algeria has kept unique traits. Since independence in 1962, Algeria has lived under the rule of a one-party system, namely the Algerian Liberation Front that led the struggle for independence, took power and controlled all government authorities as well as the country's economy. The party used its own socialist philosophy as an ideological tool to maintain power. This philosophy includes religious and Islamic values and the call for Arab solidarity.

In recent years, however, the country witnessed a steep rise in the popularity of Islamic-revivalist movements. The favorable public response to the Islamists was due to two factors:
- The first is common to all Arab republics where the socialist philosophy of the ruling parties failed to foster economic reforms and bring about real

development. The Arab defeat of 1967 in the war against Israel was a heavy blow for all Arab socialist systems and had a negative impact on the morale of all Arab countries and created a crisis of identity.
- The second factor is related to local developments in Algeria. Economic problems worsened and there was corruption among high officials in the ruling Algerian Liberation Front. The amount of money that party members have misused has reached 26 billion dollars in a time span of only 20 years. Algerian society has become divided into two classes, a ruling minority that enjoys all rights and privileges and a poor majority that suffers from economic hardships. When the party failed to bring clear and decisive answer to the economic problems, solutions proposed by Islamicist groups, headed by the Islamic Salvation Front, seemed to be the only viable alternative.

At this stage of development, the major political parties in Algeria were the National Liberation Front, the Islamic Salvation Front, the Front of Socialist Powers, and the Pro-Democracy Movement. A brief discussion of each party will clarify its specific traits and characteristics.

The National Liberation Front

As was indicated previously, the National Liberation Front is a socialist party with a preference for group leadership. The popularity of the party was derived from the decisive role it played in leading the struggle for independence against the French colonial power. This popularity has gradually declined and diminished because of weaknesses in the political party structure, widespread corruption and the failure to find solutions to rising social problems. The party became unpopular not only with segments of society outside the party, but also among party members themselves who were not satisfied with the programs, leadership and the organizational patterns of the party cells.

Originally the party monopolized all power and authority to select the national leader, the government and all top positions of economic and state-corporations. This power was gradually eroded for two reasons:
- The party itself attempted in a number of internal reforms to separate itself from the national government. These reforms aimed at abolishing the earlier practice of giving the top administrative positions of all government authorities to party members only.
- The government then took great pains to appear as an authority that operates independently from the party.

It is a well-known fact that within the National Liberation Front signs of polarization and divisions appeared, creating several internal blocks that opposed each other.

The Islamic Salvation Front

The Front was officially established in 1989 after the government opted for the multi-party system. However, its real beginning is much earlier. This was amply demonstrated during the powerful demonstrations organized by the party in 1988.

The party is administered by the Shura Council which has highly qualified people in its ranks and is aided by a very effective administration. The party is furthermore characterized by a strong sense of solidarity connecting the top and the base of the organization. It served as an umbrella organization for many intellectual trends of thought such as the Movement for Takfir and Hijrah and the Organization for Islamic Militant Struggle which is heavily influenced by Islamic militant groups of other Arab countries. Members of this organization clashed with the Liberation Front several times and their leader was killed in March 1988.

The party adopted violent struggle as its main strategy to oppose the government. It emphasizes the establishment of an Islamic state which promises to find solutions to all the pressing economic problems caused by the political and administrative corruption. People will be held accountable for their crimes. The party also advocates respect for the basic freedom of citizens; however, it does not take a clear stand on the issue of the multi-party system in case it should gain political power.

It is highly enlightening to study certain comments of the party leaders concerning this matter. Dr. Abbas Madani, the leader of the Islamic Salvation Front, pointed out: "If democracy is defined as a framework ensuring respect for public opinion, we can agree with this; however, we will not tolerate or accept any elected person who opposes Islam or does not follow the shari'a as his guidance and source of values." Ali Belhaj, the second leader of the Front, stated: "After gaining power we will only give permission to those parties that do not question the shari'a or hinder its implementation; we will forbid all parties that oppose the Islamic state and the implementation of the shari'a." These two remarks lack much needed specifications. One has to ask, what are the standards by which the party will judge what is contradictory or even hindering the implementation of the shari'a and what is not? This is a highly sensitive issue because in its light it will be decided which political party will be allowed to exist and which will be forbidden.

The Front of Socialist Powers

Hussein Ait Ahmad, one of the leader of the revolution, has established the Front of Socialist Powers in 1963. He separated from the National Liberation Front because of differences and disagreements among the revolutionary leadership. The party advocates a brand of scientific socialism which was somehow adopted to fit with the country's Islamic roots. Since the establishment of the multi-party system, it has been part of the opposition. It calls for the protection of traditional civilizations, in particular the Berber one. It refuses the policy of Arabization and calls for making the Berber language a second national language, a move which should be guaranteed by the constitution. The party usually receives strong media coverage by France which is typical of French policy before and after independence as France has traditionally supported the Berber claims and demands.

The Pro-Democracy Movement

The strength and power of this movement can largely be attributed to its leader Ahmad Bin Billa. He enjoys extraordinary popularity as a national revolutionary leader with moderate Islamic views and because he held the presidency until being ousted in 1965. Ahmad Bin Billa's goal is to take back the presidency, but only with the support of other political parties. The Movement also calls for the elimination of government corruption and the resignation of President Shadhli Bin Jadid.

Political Reforms

All political analysts on Algeria agree that political reforms began after the October riots in 1988. The Algerian people engaged in angry and violent demonstrations causing the government to declare a state of emergency. The army intervened to disperse these demonstrations and clashed with civilians. All social groups of the Algerian society expressed their outrage and dissatisfaction with the continuing economic problems and the hardships the situation placed upon the people.

The economic problems that caused the riots in 1988 can be summarized under the following points:[2]
- a continuing rise of foreign debt reaching 19 billion in 1986 and an increasing dependency upon foreign loans;

- a decrease of the per capita income of 12% in 1986, combined with a steep rise of prices of consumer goods;
- an increase of the unemployment rate from 16% to 24.5% between 1986 and 1989; by then the number of unemployed reached 1.5 million; the labor market was furthermore burdened by the challenge to absorb an additional 150,000 people annually which is the average number of young people reaching working age each year;
- the failure of the agricultural and industrial sectors to reach production targets and a decline in quality by the service sector;
- a decrease in hard currency earnings by the government and a continued decrease of income from exports, especially oil;
- an increase of the population growth rate to 3.3% during the period of 1976 till 1984.

The political authorities realized that the only way to overcome this crisis was political reform. This process was begun by proclaiming a new constitution in 1989 replacing the constitution of 1976.[3] One of the important changes was the establishment of a multi-party system, abolishing the one-party system. Article 4 of the constitution confirms that "establishing political associations and parties is an acknowledged right."

The word "socialist" describing the nation was dropped. The first article of the constitution states: "Algeria is a democratic country." The constitution of 1976 stated in one of its articles that "the Algerian government is a socialist government".

The Prime Minister is directly responsible to the People's National Council. Before this, he was only responsible to the party only.

Democratic elections were adopted as a way to transfer power. The army was stripped of its political power and its role was limited to protect national independence and sovereignty.

The Law of Political Associations was passed in July 1989, changing the political arena into a multi-party system. Then the Election Law No. 13/89 was issued in the year 1989. This law defines the basic rules for elections in Algeria, especially rules related to electing the President of the Republic.

In summary, Algeria, which has only known a one-party system since the independence in 1962, changed to a multi-party system. The nation abolished the socialist aspect of the country's economy and adapted a system of free-market economy. The choice of democratic elections as a way of political reforms was probably the most profound change. The real cause for this change was the economic crisis.

Despite the fact that the government used rather forceful measures to quell demonstrations, it quickly started to implement political reform. The situation in

Algeria can be described in the following equation: economic crisis leading to public dissatisfaction, leading to violent confrontation with the government, leading to political reforms.

The reforms, however, did not solve all the problems, although a great deal of the public dissatisfaction was caused by the failure of the one-party system to solve the economic crisis. The political reforms turned out to be merely an attempt to stop public dissatisfaction. The political environment in Algeria with all the country's economic problems and social weaknesses was not mature enough to assure the success of the democratic experiment. Instead military institutions played an increasingly political role and heavily influenced the decisions of the government. Lebset stated that the fair distribution of wealth, high income, industrialization, modernization and a high level of education are the guarantors for the continuation of democracy. In Algeria, those conditions were certainly not fulfilled.

It is also a fact that the Law of Political Parties, though allowing a multi-party system, also imposed conditions and restrictions that allow the government to powerfully intervene in the internal affairs of the party. The law states that the Minister of Interior can obtain permission from the court to stop or dissolve any party which violates the laws. If the party poses a threat to public security and order, its main representative will be notified of the court's decision to dissolve the party.[4]

The Law of the Parties was issued on April 2, 1991, and October 15, 1991, as part of the political reforms in Algeria. Its content is summarized in the following points:[5]

- elections are general, direct and secret;
- Article 2 and 28 state that the minimum age should be 18 years for the eligible voter and 21 years for candidates to the People's National Council (the parliament);
- Articles 3 and 36 state that the People's National Council is elected for a five-year term; its members are to be elected in two rounds; the winner of the first round should obtain more than 50% of the votes; in the second round the two candidates who receive the majority of the votes should compete with each other. If both receive an equal number of votes, then the elder candidate wins;
- Article 84 states that each constituency should be represented by one seat in the parliament.

Some articles in the law caused a lot of political controversy before and after the elections. The Election Law specifies the groups of people who are allowed to cast their votes by delegation. It also states that one of the spouses can vote for the other even without his or her written approval. Either the husband or the wife can simply produce the family identification card plus the two voting identification cards (Article 54) and then cast two votes. This article was fiercely opposed by the Algerian government and the various women's associations; yet, the Islamic

Salvation Front insisted on adhering to the original text of this article which was finally endorsed by the National People's Council. In Algeria, of course, it is the husband and not the wife who makes use of the right to cast a double vote for both husband and wife. The Islamic Salvation Front, thanks to its excellent organization and party discipline, succeeded in the elections of December by mobilizing all its male members to vote. Consequently, the Front succeeded in increasing the number of votes cast in its favor by 100%. When analyzing Article 54 in greater depth, a contradiction becomes apparent with Article 8 of the same law which states that the voting should be done personally. How this article can be reconciled with husbands voting for their wives is not clear at all.

An administrative committee was formed and given the task to prepare the voting lists. The head of the regional judicial council, a judge, was appointed head of the committee. The head of the regional municipal council and representatives of the governorate were appointed as members of the committee (Article 16).

The administration of each governorate undertook the task of distributing the registration cards (Article 22).

These two articles caused a great deal of controversy. Local elections that were conducted in July of 1990 allowed the Islamic Salvation Front to win 55% of the total seats of these councils. The National Liberation Front won 32% and all the other political parties only 13%. Later, when the Islamic Salvation Front won the elections of December 1991, the National Liberation Front, the Front of Socialist Powers and the Pro-Democracy Movement accused the Islamic Salvation Front of misusing these articles and electoral fraud. The three parties submitted 341 accusations of fraud that mostly concerned the way 2 million election cards were distributed.

The Election Law and subsequent reactions by the people have deepened the political crisis in Algeria. All political parties opposed the amended Law 2/4 that was passed by the Algerian People's National Council on April 2, 1991. The Islamic Salvation Front headed the opposition campaign leading to disruption and demonstrations on June 3rd, 1991 and the declaration of the state of emergency. The army intervened for a second time to restore order and security.[6]

Despite the government's later approval of the amendment to this law, the results of the June 3rd, 1991, events were as follows:
- the significant and powerful role of the army became very apparent as an independent authority from the presidency and government;
- the position of the President became dependent upon decisions made by the military leadership, instead of the government controlling the military;
- this became obvious, when the army demanded the resignation of the government of Mawlud Hamrush and requested Sayyid Ahmad Ghazali, then Minister of Interior, to head the new government;

- the military deemed these steps necessary for the sake of restoring national order and security. President Shadli Bin Jadid was forced to approved these military decisions;[7]
- the general parliamentary elections were announced to take place at the end of that year.

Process and Results of the 1991 Parliamentary Elections

On October 16, 1991, the Presidential Decree No. 91-386 was issued calling upon the electoral committees to prepare for parliamentary elections to be held on December 26, 1991. In case a second round was needed, it was to take place on January 16, 1992. The following lines are an attempt to summarize and interpret subsequent events. The author had to depend on Arabic newspapers. They were the only ones to cover the events on a daily basis. The difference in political orientation of these newspapers was taken into account and separated from factual reporting and straightforward news items.

During the first stage of the elections, 51 political parties participated with some 5800 candidates competing for 430 seats. The total number of Algerian voters participating was 7.86 million from an electorate of 13.26 million.[8]

As expected by diplomatic and political circles, the first round of the parliamentary elections resulted in a victory for the Islamic Salvation Front which gained 188 seats. The Front of Socialist Powers gained 25 seats while the National Liberation Front won only 16 seats. The rest of the parties were able to score very few places. Finally, a total of 8 parties became eligible for the second round of elections. The Islamic Salvation Front needed only 28 seats in order to achieve an absolute majority. In reality, the Front was set to score two thirds of the seats during the second round and if that had happened the ISF would have had the power and authority to amend the constitution.

The ISF victory in the first round stirred various reaction, ranging from cautious silence to firm rejection of the results. Objections grew even stronger after the ISF leaders, especially Sheikh Abdulqadir Hashami, the temporary spokesman of the Front, called upon the Algerian people "to get ready for a total change of lifestyle, including eating, drinking and clothing habits in accordance with the Islamic creed."[9] The leaders also announced that "democracy, which at its very core is a Western invention, does not really suit an Islamic social order".[10] The republican system, in their view, has no basis in Islamic legislation and religion.

On the other hand, the leading political parties showed silent dissatisfaction. Prime Minister al-Ghazali pointed out that "the so-called democratic parties in the country buried their heads in the sand during the previous months acting rather irresponsibly and now they had to pay the price".

Besides political statements, the overall reaction can be described as threefold:
- The first group called upon the people to participate in the second round of the elections; however, this group was divided in its reaction towards the victory of the ISF. The NLF, although rejecting the election results, maintained that the will of the voters had to be respected and if anybody should feel wronged he could file a legal complaint. The Front of the Socialist Forces, however, strongly opposed the ISF victory and organized a demonstration in which 300,000 people participated to express their dismay over the election results.[11]
- The second group called upon the people to boycott the second round of the parliamentary elections and thus preventing the ISF from gaining political power. This group included labor unions, the National Council for Sports, human rights organizations, the National Council for Contractors, the Algerian Union of Businessmen, the Social Pioneer Party and the Algerian Women's Association.[12]
- Military leaders formed the third group, expressing their objection to the election results in their official newspapers. The ISF was described as being "merely a tool for destroying modern Algeria". Military leaders also demanded that the second round of elections be delayed and accused President Shadli Bin Jadid of lenience towards the ISF for the sake of keeping power. This third group, the military, played an effective and powerful role in shaping events later on. It controlled most of the strategic locations in the country.

Events started to unfold rapidly when President Ash-Shadli Bin Jadid handed in his resignation on November 11, 1992. In his letter of resignation, the President stated that the "democratic practices are grossly misused in an environment filled with the bickering of political factions. In fact, the situation is so dangerous and critical that it might affect the very foundation of the country and national unity."

The letter of resignation also called for the dissolution of the National People's Council at an earlier date. When the situation worsened, the military was asked by Prime Minister al-Ghazali to take over the country. A Supreme Security Council then took full power to manage the country's affairs. Finally, the High Presidential Council was established in place of the President which was to lead the country until December 1993. The declaration of a state of emergency on February 10, 1993 brought the democratic experiment of Algeria to a grinding halt.

A Possible Interpretation of the Events

It is not an exaggeration to say that the democratic experiment in Algeria was bound to fail from its very beginning. One comes to this conclusion when taking social and economic changes and local and international developments into consideration. These circumstances caused the democratic experiment to turn into an adventure that threatened the political structure not only of Algeria, but the entire region as well; moreover, military intervention was inevitable following the events of June 3, 1991. The military leadership never even attempted to cover its dislike for the ISF which it acquired for this party ever since the violent clashes of 1988 and 1991.

The real cause behind the events of June 3, 1991, was a promise by the military to President Shadli Bin Jadid that it will intervene for the sake of protecting order and security until the end of Prime Minister al-Ghazali's term in December 1991. Al-Ghazali declared that elections would be held before the end of 1991. Although political parties were in favor of delaying the election date, it appears that the state of instability in the country and the powerful role of the army in the process of political decision making caused elections to be held according to the original schedule.

I was essential that elections be held before Prime Minister Al-Ghazali's term ended for at two reasons: no party would gain the majority which would force Prime Minister al-Ghazali to form a National Coalition Government. In this case, the democratic experiment would continue with no further authority given to the Islamicists. The second scenario widely expected was that an ISF victory in an unstable political environment together with a weak presidential authority would inevitably lead to a military intervention.

And so it happened. In order to justify military intervention, President Shadli Bin Jadid had to resign and the Algerian People's Council was dissolved. When these two conditions were met, Prime Minister al-Ghazali in accordance with the constitution was able to call on the military.

Military intervention was intended to be strong and decisive. The army leaders were certain that the reactions of the Arab and other countries would range from silent approval to cautious protest. Arab countries, in general, and Algeria's two neighbors Morocco and Tunisia in particular, knew very well that a clear victory by the ISF in the parliamentary elections of Algeria would certainly give a great boost to other prohibited Islamic movements in the region to seek power.

It should also be noted that relations with the two neighbors became very strained when Algeria allowed the leaders of the forbidden Tunisian Islamicist movement to stay on its territory enjoying the status of political refugees. The Tunisian Minister of Interior, Abdullah al-Jalal, accused the leader of the Islamicist movement of "conspiring to derail the constitution of Tunisia". The Moroccan government, in turn, accused an unspecified neighboring country of being involved in the student clashes between leftists and Islamicists in the universities of Jaddah, Dar al-Beidha, Fez and al-Qunaytarah.

There is increasing evidence of close relations and cooperation between the ISF in Algeria, the Islamic Front in Sudan, the government of Iran and the Islamic Revival Movement in Tunisia. There was indeed a strong possibility of the formation of an Islamicist triangle covering Iran, Sudan and Algeria, each promoting and spreading Islamicist ideas in its respective region. Moreover, European countries, especially France, believed that the rising Islamicist movement in Algeria will negatively affect their strategic interests. Western countries also realized the difficulties that would inevitably come up in dealing with a future Islamicist government in Algeria; therefore most countries would argue that the events in Algeria are merely an internal affair because they want to avoid the danger of an Islamicist state in their own vicinity.

1	Dr. Hasan ath-Thahir "Democracy: a Study on its Concepts, Principles, Ideological Roots and Contemporary Specification", Magazine of the Faculty of Commerce, Sanaa University, No.6 of 1986, p.102
2	Ahmad Thabit "Political Pluralism in the Arab World" in al-Mustaqbal al-Arabia, Center for the Study of Arab Unity, Beirut, Nr.55, January 1992, p.213; Nifin Abdulmun'im Mus'id "The Argument for Isolation or Participation", al-Mustaqbal al-Arabi, Center for the Study of Arab Unity, Beirut, Nr.145, March 1991, pp.65-66
3	Ahmad Thabit, p.13
4	For the text of the Law of the Parties, see: The Official Gazette of the Republic of Algers, Nr. 14 of April 3rd 1991 and Nr.48 of October 16th 1991
5	October Magazine, Nr.794, 6th year 12.10.1992, pp.4-5
6	Al-Wasat Magazine, Nr.1, 3-9 February 1992, p.15
7	Al-Alam Magazine, Nr.413, 11.1.1992, p.10 Al-Musawir Magazine, Nr.3508, 3.1.1992, pp.16-17 Akhir Sa'a Magazine, Nr.2985, p.11
8	Al-Musawir Magazine, Nr.3510, 17.1.1992, p.4
9	Akhir Sa'ah Magazine, Nr.2985, p.11
10	ibid.
11	Al-Alam Magazine, Nr.413, pp.10-11
12	Al-Musawir Magazine, Nr.3510, pp.6-7

A Critical View of the Draft Law for Elections

by Dr. Muhammad Ja'far Qasim

The introduction to this treatise deals with two distinct periods in the modern history of Yemen. The first begins with the foreign colonial occupation of Yemen in the 19th Century, namely the Ottoman Turkish occupation of the former north until the rise of the Yemen Arab Republic (1879 - 1962) and the British occupation of the former south until the proclamation of the People's Democratic Republic of Yemen (1839 - 1967). The second begins in the second half of the 20th Century with the rise of the two Yemeni republics and ends with the re-unification and emergence of the Republic of Yemen (1962 - 1990).

The Period Preceding the Establishment of the two Yemeni Republics

The northern part of the country was under Ottoman-Turkish occupation between 1882 and 1918 AD. The people resisted foreign occupation and Yemen became known as the "graveyard of the invaders". Some historical publications mention the fact that the Ottoman Empire allocated a certain number of seats in its parliament in Istanbul for representatives from Yemen. Further studies need to be carried out on the representation of Yemen in the Ottoman parliament. The range of duties and rights of the Yemeni representatives in question should be identified and the impact they had on the Turkish government should be clarified. Let us hope that Yemeni historians and lawyers will shed more light on this interesting historical fact.

During the period of the Mutawakkilite Kingdom (1918 - 1962), Yemen did not have any kind of parliamentary representation. Oppression, tyranny and an absolute system of government was prevalent instead. The Yemeni opposition movement represented by the Free Yemenis (Ahrar Al-Yaman) called for the formation of a legislative council based on the principles of free elections. The council was to be formed preliminary by assigned members. Later, once a higher political awareness had been achieved among the population, free elections were to be held as stated in the Holy National Charter.

During the period of British occupation (1839 - 1967) the southern part of the country was ruled by the British colonial power. The British faced continuous opposition from the people, ultimately resulting in the outbreak of the 14th of October Revolution in 1963 which eventually achieved national independence on November 30, 1967.

In its first century of occupation, the colonial rulers imposed severe restrictions on the pursuit of any political activities by the people. No representational organizations were established during this period. This fact is highlighted by the French political magazine Articles and Documents, which reads on page 18 of issue 1786: "During an entire century, life in Aden was a boring and monotonous routine with only very few stimulations. The population was severely curtailed in the pursuit of any political activities." However, starting in 1937, the colonial administration began applying the same institutional policy which was practiced in other British colonies before their independence.

A Legislative Council was established for the first time in Aden in 1947 which totaled 16 members. Half the number was nominated from among government employees and the other half from non-government employees. In 1955, the number of Council members was raised to 18. Again, half was selected from governmental organizations, and the other half from non-governmental organizations. At the same time, a first attempt to introduce elections was made by having three members elected from non-governmental organizations and a fourth member by the Crater Municipal Council. In legal terms, however, these elections fell into the category of restrictive voting which tied the right to vote to the financial income of the voter. Women were also prohibited from voting. The most severe restrictions were placed upon Yemenis not born in Aden. They were barred from exercising any political rights which, on the other hand, were readily granted to other residents of the British colony, even if they were not born in Aden. This situation caused a majority of the people, who technically possessed all the qualifications necessary for voting, to boycott elections.

In 1958, the number of the Legislative Council members was raised to 23. 12 members were elected on the basis of very restrictive voting terms similar to those set down in 1955, but with the financial condition reduced to a lesser amount. The elections taking place in 1959 were boycotted for the same reasons as the previous ones.

In 1962, the number of Council members from among the non-governmental employees was raised to 16 from a total of 23 members; however, the same restrictive voting terms remained and the following elections in 1964 were again boycotted.

The voting system in all three elections was a one-round-majority election. The same system was applied in the United Kingdom. By continually boycotting elections, the Yemeni people put the election process in a rather paradoxical situation, because the result was that the body of voters basically consisted of foreigners. The percentage of participants actually declined over the three elections periods in question. The number of voters in 1955 amounted to 4971. In 1959 there were 6000 electors and in 1964 again 6000. Only foreigners were satisfied with the existing rules and endeavored to take maximum advantage of the situation. The fact that a certain Mr. Goshin of Hindu origin and Joseph Salos, a Christian of Somali origin, both received a majority of votes, is ample proof that most voters came from the non-Yemeni segments of society.

In areas outside Aden, no public elections were held, though the 1951 constitution of Lahij called for the election of a legislative council for the Fadhli Sultanate. Eventually a legislative council was in fact established following a decree issued in 1963. Its members were elected by restrictive voting procedures.

The Election Laws of the two Republics of Yemen (1962 - 1990)

In each of the former Republics of Yemen (the Yemen Arab Republic and the People's Democratic Republic of Yemen) a number of election laws were passed. In Sana'a, a total of four laws were issued:
- Republican Decree No.1 of 1971 regarding the election of the Shura Council
- Law No.8 of 1975 regarding elections themselves
- Law No.29 of 1980
- Law No.22 of 1988, which is an amendment of Law No.29 of 1980

In Aden, the following two laws were issued:
- Law No.18 of 1978 regarding the election of the People's Supreme Council
- Law No.9 of 1989 regarding the election of the People's Council.

The following will attempt to briefly analyze and evaluate these six election laws. It will furthermore serve as an introduction to the most recent election laws passed in the present Republic of Yemen.

All the Yemeni election laws (except Law No.1 of 1971, which was issued in Sana'a and opted for indirect elections on three levels) are based on modern principles of democracy. They call for public elections to be conducted in line with the principles of equality, freedom and privacy.

All the laws agree to grant voting rights to each Yemeni citizen at the age 18 and above. They differ in regard to the conditions of how Yemeni citizenship has been obtained. The Law issued in Aden excludes any reference related to the holders of Yemeni nationality; however, Laws No.8 and 29 of 1975 and 1980 issued in Sana'a specify a minimal time period for holding Yemeni citizenship before the citizen can fully pursue his political rights. Law No.8 of 1975 requires a minimum period of 5 years of citizenship, while Law No.29 of 1980 even requires a period of 10 years.

All laws require the formation of a Supreme Election Committee appointed by the presidency and of other committees to prepare, manage and supervise the election process.

The election laws differ in terms of the conditions to be fulfilled by prospective candidates. The law issued in Aden stipulates that the candidate must be 24 years of age or older. He must not have been involved in any anti-revolutionary activities during the 26th of September and 14th of October Revolutions. He should be loyal to the constitution, lead an exemplary personal and professional life and be capable of reading and writing. The laws of 1975 and 1980 issued in Sana'a stipulate that the candidate should be at least 25 years of age, capable of reading and writing, have proper behavior and observe religious practices. No one can be a candidate if he has previously been sentenced for election fraud or other criminal behavior that throw doubts on his honesty.

All laws agree that the government should bear the costs incurred in the process of the elections. They also demand the formation of exactly 'equal' electorates. Exceptions are Law No.18 of 1978 which states that the administrative unit should also be the electorate regardless of the number of inhabitants. Laws No.8 and No.29 of 1975 and 1980 allow for a variation of plus/minus 10% among the different electorates. Laws No.8 and No.29 issued in 1975 and 1980 opt for the system of a one-round majority election, while Law No.9 of 1989 prefers the system based on an exclusive list of a two-round majority election.

The Laws of 1978 and 1989 do not mention a second round of elections in case the first one results in an insufficient number of candidates with an absolute majority. This problem actually came up when complementary elections were organized for three vacant seats in the Aden governorate shortly before the re-unification of Yemen. None of the three candidates could obtain an absolute majority and the three seats remained vacant until re-unification.

The laws of 1975, 1980 and 1989 place the responsibility of dealing with appeals upon the judiciary, while the law of 1978 gives this responsibility to the election committees. All laws agree to grant to the legislative body the power to decide on matters of candidacy and membership. The rules and regulations issued in Law No.9 of 1989 were not applied to any public elections and remained mere theories.

A Critical View of the Draft Law

The Election Law of 1992

The law consists of 79 articles which can be arranged under the following eight headings:
- the right to vote and definitions
- voters' lists
- the Supreme Election Committee
- organization and rules of campaigning
- election procedures
- appeals
- crimes
- general transitional regulations.

In the following section the most important regulations of the draft law for the parliamentary elections in the Republic of Yemen will be presented. Following this, an attempt will be made to evaluate the law based on the following criteria:
- the historical context of the draft law
- the principle of competitive elections
- the organization of the voters
- distribution of the electorates
- organization of actual balloting
- election system
- neutrality of the government and its organizations
- decisions taken concerning election disputes

Illuminating the historical context of the draft law means specifying earlier laws which served as sources for those writing the new laws.

It is quite obvious that the Constitution of the Republic and Election Law No.29 of 1980, based on Law No.8 of 1975, both issued in Sana'a, represent the main historical sources for the new draft law. In fact, all articles of Law No.29 of 1980 were more or less incorporated in the new law with only a few amendments. The sole major disparity between the two is that Law No.29 of 1980 advocates an individual voting system with a majority election in two rounds.

Other updated articles are related to chapter 4 of the draft law, concerning the organization and control of election campaigning. The same holds true for the articles of section 1/chapter 6 concerning accusations and appeals prior to handing out winning certificates and the articles of chapter 8 regarding transitional regulations. The articles of chapter 4 of the new draft law are the same as those adopted in other democratic countries, yet the articles of section 1/chapter 6 concerning appeals are all taken from the rules of the Constitution of the Republic of Yemen which calls for the Supreme Court to decide on these matters. Finally, the articles of chapter 8 concerning general and transitional rules address our specific political circumstances. They call for conducting elections before the end of the transition period.

The Principles of Competitive Elections

Competitive elections are assured by the national constitution which acknowledges the multi-party system. Politically, Yemen can be described as a multi-party society where freedom of opinion is universally advocated and implemented. A multi-party society is characterized by a freely expressed variety of ideas. It allows free assembly where the different ideas, even if they should be critical of the ruling system, can be discussed openly. It also guarantees the freedom to associate with political parties and participate in their activities. Members of parliament are free to form different interest groups and political alliances.

The constitutional system of the Republic of Yemen is based on a multi-party political society which is guaranteed by the constitution and other relevant laws, especially those dealing with journalism and political parties. In addition, the draft law explicitly allows the political parties and organizations to participate in managing the elections on various levels, thus ensuring the proper flow of the electoral process.

Organization of Election Campaigns by the Candidates

The law guarantees the right of any citizen fulfilling certain conditions to run for parliament. This is a confirmation of the existence of personal freedom. The conditions for candidates for parliamentary membership are defined in articles 41 and 43 of the draft law. Article 41 deals with the age, nationality, literacy and personal behavior of the candidate. These conditions fall in line with the conditions stipulated in the constitution.

Article 46 prohibits certain persons, such as the governors to provinces, from proclaiming themselves to be candidates. This prohibition is to avoid any force or pressure which could possibly be levied upon the voter.

Article 43 stipulates that an independent candidate should obtain the support of at least 300 voters in his electorate. The objective of this condition is to ensure the effectiveness of the candidacy. In some countries the candidates have to deposit a certain amount of money which is only refunded if the candidate wins the election. The last paragraph of this article does oblige the candidate to fulfill certain financial commitments. This section should be changed since it will only curtail the freedom of candidacy and make it depend upon monetary considerations.

The proper way of announcing one's candidacy is defined in article 42. An application by the candidate needs to be handed to the election committee. In this article, the word committee has an ambiguous meaning. Here, committee most probably means the Supreme Election Committee, since this article is taken from article 29 of Law No.29 of 1980. A better definition of the word committee is very much needed. Candidates are announced to the public by a process which makes known the candidate's name, profession and qualifications, enabling the voters to properly select the candidates of their choice.

Equality in Campaigning

Chapter 4 deals with the organization of the election campaign. It identifies the places where election posters can be put up. Article 35 regulates the distribution of voters' political programs and other publications until a certain specified date before the actual ballot day.

Article 37 identifies certain public places where election posters are forbidden to be put up, such as mosques and educational centers. In those places, campaigning is prohibited.

Article 37 obliges the candidates to hold election assemblies for the presentation of their programs. The candidates and their programs have to be introduced to the voters. Here we realize the importance of equal access to public facilities by candidates for such purposes. The impact of traditional means of campaigning is very low compared with advanced audio-visual means such as radio television.

In Yemen, radio and television stations are considered public facilities owned by the government. It is of utmost importance to allow candidates equal use of these facilities during the campaigning period. Despite the powerful impact of these media, the draft law lacks clarification concerning the use of mass media by candidates for presenting their programs and ideas.

In Yemen, it is difficult to solve this issue due to the large number of parties. Nevertheless, an equal time period should be assigned to each party to allow a number of candidates from different electorates, e.g. for each party at least 50 candidates in 50 electorates, to present themselves in radio and television.

Article 31 specifies that the formal period for campaigning should be the two weeks prior to balloting day. During this formal period all candidates can equally gain access to campaigning facilities provided by the government through the Supreme Election Committee. The duration of this period seems reasonable for introducing the candidate to the voters, but this does not mean that parties and independent candidates can only campaign during these two weeks. It is possible to pursue earlier campaigning, since no objections to this are defined in the draft law.

Organization of the Voters

The requirements specified by the draft law for obtaining the right to vote are stated in article 2 and concern nationality and age.

The right of election is restricted to Yemeni nationals, excluding foreigners living in the country. This is an internationally applied rule. The draft law furthermore distinguishes between native born Yemenis and those who obtain Yemeni citizenship. This distinction became necessary because the law requires a time period preceding the acquisition of Yemeni citizenship. During this period the new citizen has to prove his allegiance to Yemen. Concerning the length of the time period, the draft law refers to the Law of Nationality, thus avoiding any contradiction between the two laws.

Article 2 stipulates that the elector should be at least 18 years of age which is the same as the age of 'maturity' according to civil law. This is in line with the laws in most democratic countries. Thus the right to vote is given to each Yemeni citizen, male and female, who fulfills these two conditions. In addition to these two conditions, other criteria pertain to organizational matters. Anybody wishing to exercise his right to vote should first fulfill these preconditions. For this purpose, voters' lists are compiled consisting of the names of qualified voters. Registering one's name on the list is a basic requirement in order to exercise one's right to vote. The electoral list does not grant the right to vote, but simply functions as a proof of conditions fulfilled. Consequently, the lists can be amended quite easily in accordance with the changing profile of the electorate. In practice, these lists are revised once a year. Each voter has the right to challenge its validity in court. The draft law in chapter 2 (articles 6 - 17) is quite detailed in this regard therefore, there is no need for further comment on this matter, except maybe one further point the issue of article 14 regarding the term "district court". This term contradicts with our judicial system, which divides the courts into those of the first instance, and then courts of appeal on the provincial level, and finally the Supreme Court. For this reason there is a suggestion to change the expression "district court" to "court of the first instance".

Article 3 of the draft law restricts the right to vote for those sentenced by criminal law for 'larger offenses' or for criminal acts offending human dignity and honor. The same holds true for those lacking the legal qualifications to enjoy civil and political rights. There is nothing to be added except the necessity of defining the concept of "larger offenses" in the Criminal Law of united Yemen which is expected to be issued soon.

Article 4 of the draft law grants the voter the right to cast his vote in his place of birth. If he does not want to do so, he has to select another location for voting. Article 1 has defined that other possible locations are the voter's current place of residence, his place of work, or his place of birth, even though he might no longer live there.

Division of the Electorates

In accordance with the constitution, the draft law suggests the division of the Republic of Yemen into electorates. These electorates should have an equal number of inhabitants with a possible deviation of plus/minus 5%.

The draft law puts the total number of electorates in the whole republic at 301.

Deciding upon the exact border of these electorates is the task of the Supreme Election Committee (SEC). It has to be done with the help of figures gained from the last population census.

Article 20 of the draft law enumerates the legal conditions to be fulfilled by the members of the SEC. By giving the SEC the power and authority to divide the country into electorates combined with other forms of authority, the draft law aims at ensuring an honest and just voting process.

Organization of the Balloting

Article 40 defines the actual balloting as being public, secret, free, direct and equal. The law does not require the provision of a financial sum or a certain level of education by the electors. It also does not distinguish between male and female. Equal rights without regard to sex is guaranteed.

Article 55 ensures confidentiality of balloting, defining detailed procedures. It defines the right of the elector to select the candidate of his choice. It is also his right to put a blank paper in the balloting box or not to participate in the voting at all, in which case he should not fear criminal prosecution. Article 69 defines the penalties for anyone who infringes upon the freedom of citizens to vote.

The draft law specifies direct elections meaning that the elector should vote himself for the candidate he believes to be qualified. Equal voting means that each elector should give one vote and electors should not be discriminated against according to their educational level or for any other reason. This issue is clearly addressed in article 5 of the draft law.

The Electoral System within the Draft Law

Concerning electoral systems, it might be sufficient to mention the most important ones only. Systems range from individual voting to choosing from a party list. This can be done on a majority basis or on a representational basis. The Yemeni laws of the last six elections have covered most of the above mentioned systems, except the one based on relative representation. The two laws of 1975 and 1980 issued in Sanaa opt for the individual voting system with a single majority vote. However, the law of 1978, also issued in Sanaa, prefers a voting system based on an exclusive list with a two round majority. The law of 1989 issued in Aden has considered both individual voting and exclusive listing with two round majority voting.

Each of the above systems has its own advantages and disadvantages. For example, the relative representation system is more just in representing the various segments of society, but its main drawback lies in the difficulty to secure a stable majority for a smoothly functioning government. This inability exposes the country to recurrent political crisis.

Despite the fact that the system of majority voting has the clear advantage of easily rallying support for a government, its main weakness is that a lot of votes are wasted. The draft law opts for the individual voting system with a two-round majority vote as defined in article 60 which states the following:
- The electee is not considered a winner in an election unless he obtains an absolute majority of the votes cast in his electorate.
- If none of the candidates is able to obtain the majority as specified in the above paragraph, a complementary election (second round) should be organized in a decision to be taken by the SEC within the following 21 days after the voting day. This second round of elections should be limited to the

two candidates with the largest number of votes during the first round of elections.

The candidate who obtains the majority of votes in the second round of elections is the winner. In case both candidates obtain an equal number of votes, the Supreme Election Council should cast lots between them and thus determine the winner. The last paragraph of article 27 states that only one candidate from each electorate should enter parliament. The individual voting system with two-round majority voting as stated in the draft law seems to be suitable to our local conditions. It will most likely result in the formation of a strong and stable government. Because of the recent unification of the republic, a stable government is of prime importance. It will help in overcoming obstacles which might hamper government attempts to rule according to laws and regulations. Furthermore, the draft law requires the candidate to announce his party affiliation or run as an independent. He should disclose his political identification. This falls in line with the new multi-party system. It is only recently that we have had a multi-party system and the method of relative majority in the two rounds is not very helpful. The first round allows each party to have a chance at winning, while the second round allows for the association and coalition of different political parties with close or common political ideas and programs to promote a certain candidate.

Neutrality of the Government and its Organizations during the Election Process

Undoubtedly, non-interference by the government and former organizations in the electoral process will ensure the smooth elections. The draft law gives the duty of supervising, managing and controlling the election operations to the Supreme Election Committee. It also gives the SEC the authority to establish a number of sub-committees to run the election process, all controlled by the SEC. The main condition of membership in the SEC and other sub-committees, as stated by the draft law, is neutrality in political affiliation. This means that a member of any committee must not be a member in any political party or organization.

The SEC consists of at least 5 members appointed by presidential decree. The subcommittees of the SEC will be formed by the SEC itself. The draft law gives a wide range of power and authority to the SEC such as the division of the electorates, as defined in article 23 a, authority to issue regulations, decrees and the final announcement of the election results.

The following remarks concern the various election committees:

- It is better to delete the word "hegemony" mentioned in article 23 regarding the powers of the SEC. Instead, the word "supervision" fits much better with the rules of this law. The term "hegemony" implies control by force and has a negative connotation.
- All members of the various election committees should profess their political neutrality.
- The expression "the Supreme Election Committee controls the results of the election operations" stated in article 62 should be replaced with "the SEC writes the minutes of the results of the election operations", which is closer to the actual task of the SEC.

Decisions on Electoral Disputes (Appeals)

There is a need to assign a competent authority for dealing with possible disputes that might arise in the process of holding the elections. There are two possible institutions to whom this authority could be delegated:
- Authority could be given to a judicial authority, which is the more logical and reasonable way of dealing with appeals. Solving legal disputes is basically a judiciary matter. In countries such as the United Kingdom, the normal courts are called upon to decide in disputes related to elections.
- Another possibility is to give authority to a political body. The elected parliament is given the power to decide on the appeals raised by its members. This system is based on the principle of the "people ruling over people", giving the power of judgment to the parliament without involving the judiciary at all.

The Yemeni election law adopts the second model because it gives the elected legislative body the power to take the final decisions on disputes related to the election process. The laws issued in 1975 and 1980 in Sanaa envisioned a Supreme Court commissioned by the Legislative Council for dealing with such appeals and then presenting the results to the Council which then has the power to take the final decision.

The draft law distinguishes two categories of disputes. The first concerns disputes relating to the candidate's membership in parliament which will be the responsibility of the parliament itself once the Supreme Court has investigated the matter and presented its findings to the parliament (articles 66 and 67). The second type of appeals deal with the process and organization of the election, which is the responsibility of the Supreme Court as defined in articles 63 and 65 of the constitution.

There is, of course, the possibility of confusion between the concepts of "the candidate's rightful membership in parliament" and the "process and organization of the elections". Judicial investigations of the Supreme Court and the procedures taken by Parliament should be sufficient to settle all election disputes.

Part III

Guarantees for the Future of Democracy in Yemen

Selected papers of a two-day seminar sponsored by the People's General Congress / District 2 of the Capital, May 17-18, 1992 in Sanaa

Contemplations on Unification and Democracy in Yemen

by Dr. Ahmad Al-Wada'i

Originally I intended to apologize for not participating in this seminar and just listen to the discussions. However, my curiosity has finally overcome my reluctance, and now I find myself writing down some ideas, questions and remarks about the young democracy in Yemen. In my opinion, democracy has surprised us, the Yemeni people. Almost overnight we found ourselves living in a society that approves a multi-party system which was absolutely forbidden only yesterday. The rapid unfolding of the unification process hardly allowed us to regain our breaths and get ready for democracy and its requirements.

After unification, a volcano of political parties erupted on Yemeni soil. Over 40 parties came up, expressing a long-standing thirst for democracy. This thirst is normal after living in an atmosphere of arbitrariness and despotism for such a long time. The political fragmentation we are experiencing is an expression of this thirst, and not a sign of division or fragmentation within our society. The phenomenon of an excessive number of parties, which we are witnessing at the moment, is a temporary one and will not last for a long time.

Questions to Our Newborn Democracy

After these introductory thoughts, I shall now raise some important and urgent questions concerning our newborn democratic experience. What we are experiencing now is practical and applied democracy that started two years ago. Its exact birthday coincides with the day of national unification on May 22, 1990. Yet we have to ask ourselves, is the Yemeni mentality capable of clearly comprehending the historic significance of this sudden appearance of democracy?

In order to illuminate this question further, let me remind you of the following facts: The current democratic developments in our country are moving under a liberal banner. Political slogans and symbols are exactly in accordance with liberal thinking. We all the typical signs of a liberal democracy, such as a multi-party system, the peaceful transfer of power, the principle of law and order (the state being under the rule of the law), separation of the state powers, equal political rights, respect of human rights and that all government authorities are subject to law and legislation, etc.

Here we need to remember the historic and social roots of liberal democracy. Liberal democracy came into existence by way of political evolution within a capitalist system, and was first realized in Europe. Democracy grew and developed within a distinct class, namely the bourgeois class, playing a dominating role over the last three centuries in European history.

Given all these facts, one may have some serious questions about the possibility of implementing liberal democracy in our country with its very specific and unique circumstances. Do we realize what is specific and what is general about this type of democracy? And even before trying to answer this question, we have to ask ourselves, what is it which made us select this particular color or shape of our political system? We might also wonder if we have any alternatives or options to our present choice.

Studying liberal democracy in its original home, Europe, we discover a long and troubled history, beginning with the Renaissance and the Religious Reformation, followed by the era of Enlightenment. Then where is the renaissance in Yemen? Where is our era of religious reformation and enlightenment?

We should ask ourselves furthermore, will Yemen be required to pass through these eras all at once? Or is it not necessary at all for us to go through the same stages of European development after accepting the liberal democratic system?

Marriage between Unification and Democracy

Now let us move from these issues of general concern to the specific ones, stemming from the unique circumstances of Yemeni society. We certainly find a long list of problems and issues, which we as Yemenis tend to avoid or even ignore altogether for one reason or another.

In the following lines, we will list some of these specific issues. We all know that the unification acted as the "midwife" to the birth of democracy in Yemen. Before unification, our people lived in two different states, ruled by two different governments, which were organized in accordance with two different political structures. These two political systems were completely opposite to the point of even contradicting each other. Only complete unification could possibly solve this contradiction. For the actual implementation of unification there was no other alternative except democracy as the means to prevent each side from trying to swallow the other. The idea of simply taking over the other side proved to be unrealistic during the violent conflicts of the seventies. Coming to terms with each other was only possible through unification, which in turn could only happen on the foundation of democracy. Thus, our national unification would have been impossible without the introduction of democracy.

The question to be asked here is the following: For how long is unification in need of democracy? There is no guarantee that this happy marriage between unification and democracy will last forever. Judging from our present reality and past experiences, our country might try to walk with one leg again, finding itself with unification, but without democracy.

We should ask ourselves if we really know the point at which the two dear friends "unification and democracy" could possibly part. Even more important is the question, how can we prepare ourselves for meeting such a challenge and keep the marriage together?

Everybody agrees that unification is our final and irrevocable choice, with no second thoughts allowed under any circumstances. But this endorsement that unification has acquired from all sides with an absolute majority was not given to democracy. Democracy is clearly the weaker part in this relationship.

This observation is furthermore confirmed by the events surrounding the two issues of democracy and unification. Is it not a fact that we are getting rid of the remnants of our national division much faster than our heritage of despotism and arbitrariness? This may be considered normal because the Yemeni mentality is very much aware of the national division and segregation. It does not hold the same level of awareness of despotism and the lack of democracy. This can be explained by the long period of history when Yemen languished under despotic regimes. The experience of national division was relatively short and never accepted as part of our lives. Despotism, on the other hand, has deep roots within ourselves and thus is taken as a sort of inevitability.

Before ending these contemplations, I have to make clear that the newborn democracy in Yemen is not just an accidental offshoot of the process of unification. Democracy in Yemen is much older than that and has always been a pivotal point of attention in the long history of the Yemeni liberation movements.

We should really delve much deeper into our specific and unique problems of democracy, but time is running short. Therefore, I will merely summarize my thoughts.

There is definitely a close relationship between the social, economic and religious structures of any society and its particular development of democracy. This relationship is a fact proved by social sciences and our society is no exception.

Then which kind of democracy fits with our particular society? Which type do we want to adopt for our country? How can this democracy harmonize with the political, economic and religious structures in Yemen? Do we know the points of contact where these structures can meet and interact successfully with the new concept of democracy? What can we do to make these points of interaction fruitful?

Third-World Democracies and the New World Order

by Dr. Mansur Aziz az-Zindani

Among those international variables considered important for political development, especially after the failure of the previous system of international relations, democracy is placed on the top of the list as an effective ingredient for the new system. This new system of international relations, which has been termed the "new world order", is presently being established on the ruins of the Cold War Era that followed World War II. Advocates of this new order suggest that democracy, which succeeded in their own societies, will surely achieve the same level of success in other countries. Therefore, all that needs to be done by these other societies is to accept and believe in democracy as the ideology of our present age, and peace and stability will be achieved more or less automatically. This "cure of all ailments" will be effective within the boundaries of the country and among the nations all over the world.

The countries of the southern hemisphere, the so called "South" or "Third World", are strongly influenced by, and to some extent exert influence on, current world affairs. Some of these countries have welcomed and accepted the concept of democracy as an effective remedy for achieving internal stability on one hand and to please the developed countries, the leaders of the "new world order", on the other hand.

The initial welcome with which some countries of the South received the powerful phenomenon of democracy, comes from hoping that this would be the much-needed remedy to achieve their political, economic, cultural and social goals while getting rid of political corruption from which they have been suffering for the past decades. Yet these understandable ambitions and hopes will face stiff challenges internally and externally.

Challenges to our Young Democracy

The following lines focus on the external challenges that threaten the newborn democracies of the developing countries. Hopefully, there will be other papers dealing with the internal challenges as well.

The following thoughts are meant to deepen the awareness of those concerned with and responsible for democracy's implementation and call upon them to exert their utmost efforts for protecting the young democracies in their respective countries. Only then will it be possible to achieve positive results benefiting the nations of our region. And let us not forget, there will be keen observers of the democratic process in the southern countries who will not hesitate for one minute to interfere directly or indirectly for the sake of giving these young democracies an orientation which suits their own purposes and interests. The policies adopted by the countries advocating the "new world order" already show tendencies in that direction.

Defending our Democracy from the Big Friends

To counter tendencies of interference by our "big friends", this paper will bring up a number of thoughts for contemplation:
- The political elite of the Third World countries are confused as to which pattern of democracy to adopt.
- The developed countries are not concerned at all with the desires and wishes of the Third World countries.
- The dependency of the southern countries on the north in the areas of economy, culture, military, education and information will continue; this will curtail the freedom of those countries of making their own decisions in matters of international policy.
- The adoption of a certain type of democracy imposed by the developed countries upon the weaker southern ones will result in the slow erosion of the national and regional identity.
- This erosion of the national and regional identity in the southern countries will disturb their original pattern of life and long-cherished traditions; fundamental change in the social, economic and cultural fabric will occur, shaping the political affairs of the nations in the developing world.
- Disturbance of the cultural, economic, social and political structures will create social instability, which in turn threatens the very existence of democracy.

These are some thoughts on the worldwide phenomena of democratization. For the sake of shedding more light on these previous points, let me add the following:
- The new world order consists of developed nations, countries surrounding these nations and marginal countries.
- The southern countries are characterized by similar political, economic, cultural and social circumstances.
- The relationship between the developed nations and the developing world can take the form of mutual reliance, subordination by the weaker or full independence.
- Democracy can assume various manifestations. It is important to analyze each type of democracy and the means through which a particular manifestation can be implemented in the context of another country.
- Democracy should be able to guarantee political, economic and social stability.
- Interference by the developed nations in the process of democratic development of the weaker countries happens because of different motivations. These include: to subordinate the weaker countries, to support certain local political groups against others, or even to curb the development of democracy by adopting a policy of restricting democratic change. The last mentioned, ironically, seems likely to ultimately lead to the imposition of dictatorship.

Safeguarding the Future of Democracy in Yemen

by Dr. Muhammad Ahmad As-Saidi

As soon as we began the countdown for ending the transitional period (from unification to parliamentary elections), much discomfort was voiced by various political and social forces, all worrying about the future of democracy. It is an anxiety that grows on the assumption that the Yemeni society is not yet prepared or qualified to adopt a life of freedom on the basis of a democratic system. The factors responsible for this, they argue, are social, political and economic. They add that the main obstacle to the implementation of full democracy, however, is the tribal structure of our society, combined with a backward economy and regional sensitivities.

Based on these assumptions, those pessimistic voices expect that whoever wins the elections will ultimately overturn democratic practices and return to a one-party system. The winner will do so by exclusively promoting those to leading positions who are absolutely loyal to the ruling party. These pessimistic voices also imply that in case the results of the elections indicate a change in the current political power constellation, this would stir much regional sensitivities and cause tribal turmoil. In order to avoid these complications several possible remedies are suggested:
- The creation of a Charter of Political Behavior which would be binding for all political parties after being signed by them.
- The prolongation of the current transition period or the institution of another. The current coalition between the two ruling parties (PGC and YSP) would basically continue but some representatives of other parties would be included as well.
- The creation of an Advisory Council that should consist mainly of tribal or regional representatives of those political forces that lost in the parliamentary elections and include members of academia. Some members of this council would be elected, while the rest would be appointed. The goal of the Council would be easing regional sensitivities and creating a social equilibrium. It would also have a monitoring function for the parliament in case the

body included among its ranks representatives who were not especially well qualified in their professional and academic background. This Advisory Council would have the right to voice its views on some or most important political issues.
- The breakup of centralization by distributing political power and supporting the local government through the election of local councils.

Understanding democracy

Before penetrating further into the topic, and in order to give complete treatment to the problems, it is necessary to agree on a common definition of democracy. Democracy here means a parliamentary democracy based on an applied constitution as is the case in the so-called free world. This parliamentary democracy includes the following points:
- A constitutional government where the ruler derives his mandate from free and direct elections after presenting himself to the people with a clear political program based on the principles of his party. The ruler also willingly and peacefully accepts his removal from office according to rules fixed by the constitution.
- The law rules supremely, the constitution is fully respected, and there is independence for judiciary is guaranteed. No judge can be removed from his position or transferred to another area without a decision made by the judiciary itself. A constitutional court is established that adjudicates cases of wrongful application of laws. The court is responsible for solving constitutional differences between the various elected councils and the government.
- Elected councils represent the people, such as the Council of Deputies, the National Council, or the People's Council. They are elected in direct and free elections. Similar councils are established on the level of the province and directorate (district), and are also elected in free and direct elections. In order to achieve this, all citizens must enjoy equal rights in casting their votes and becoming candidates without being restricted by any form of discrimination. Each candidate also has the right to campaign openly in order to win the confidence of the voters. These councils are given the full powers of legislation and the right to observe and, if necessary, rectify government performances.
- Freedom of political expression by the various parties.

- Freedom of information including free reporting without censorship in newspapers and other mass media. This also includes the freedom to gather, establish associations, and organize peaceful demonstrations.

The full implementation of democracy inevitably leads to the abolition of class differences and establishes equality among the people. It also puts an end to amassing political power by a minority over a majority because there cannot be democracy without political freedom.

No Democracy without Political Freedom

If political freedom is granted only half heartedly, there is no way to avoid violation of the following:
- Personal freedom which includes freedom of opinion and expression of this opinion by various means and without being watched and controlled by the state apparatus. It also includes the freedom to criticize within the framework of the law and without violating the freedom of others. It guarantees the individual that he will not be imprisoned or forcefully removed from his residence. He will be allowed to move freely from one place to another, except if he has violated the law. He feels his life and dignity are secure and safe and he is never humiliated by state power. His property is safeguarded and his sources of income are not threatened. He should not be removed from his place of work because of his political affiliation and he has the right to occupy all government positions without being subjected to favoritism. The only reason for promotion at work is his personal qualification and ability.
- The right of the people to form any unarmed association or political party pursuing peaceful goals. They can also meet freely at public and private places without being subjected to government control. They can organize peaceful demonstrations and choose freely the type of government and governing administration and they can withdraw the confidence from those elected government officials. All forms of discrimination should stop, no matter if this discrimination is based on hereditary reasons, such as nobility or royalty, or on economic or religious grounds.
- No special class or group of people should be able to monopolize political power. The same holds true for certain segments of society or tribes. Instead, the choice of the majority has to be applied no matter what this choice might be.

Democracy is a complicated web of political rules that cannot be divided into different parts. Without applying it fully and completely it cannot be really called democracy and is almost certain to fail.

We the people of Yemen, have several experiences in trying to implement a partial democracy. Each time we justified it by calling it "gradual implementation" according to our social, political and economic circumstances. However in retrospect it becomes clear that these kinds of experiments did not advance us even one step. On the contrary, partial implementation of democracy in itself became a major obstacle to democratic development.

Partial implementation can never give us the guarantees for establishing a lasting democratic society. Prolonging the transition period or beginning a second one before holding elections actually means keeping the previous coalition while including some of the other political parties.

Other suggestions propose the creation of an Advisory Council or Shura Council representing the various regions and tribes. This council could also include important personalities who lost during the parliamentary elections. If all of these steps are undertaken before free elections are held, it really comes down to favoring one group of people above the other. This would constitute a gross neglect of the most basic principles of democracy and contradict the principles of freedom and equality, thus undermining the very essence of democracy.

Such undertakings are by no means suitable to advance the cause of democracy. We have already experienced two years of the transition period and it is quite clear that any extension that is not based on the will of the people expressed by way of the ballot box will inevitably play a negative role, and even grow into a further obstacle, for the implementation of democracy. More divisions will occur in the midst of our society and the old ones will deepen.

Furthermore, our citizens today are in ever increasing need of effective measures in the area of economic development. We cannot afford to continue having our strength consumed by further transition periods. The last thing this new transitional government will be thinking of is the economy of the country.

A Charter of Political Conduct might have some positive effects. However, by itself it can never guarantee the smooth development of democracy. It may have all the noble and beautiful principles one can think of, but they are mere expressions of goodwill put on paper. They will never have the authority of the constitution or the laws. The implementation of such a charter ultimately depends upon voluntary action by the parties. It is quite easy for a the party winning the elections to silently forget about this charter. Therefore, the real guarantees for the sound development of democracy must be anchored in the constitution and the laws. Only then can political parties be expected to abide by them.

The Right Time for Democracy in Yemen

Those who ask for a prolongation of the transition period maintain that the Yemeni society is not qualified yet to implement full democracy because of social, economic and political reasons. Two of the most important reasons mentioned in this context are the tribal structure and regional fragmentation. Being an economist, I believe that democracy will be the remedy for all social and political and economic ailments. Democracy is not necessarily tied to economic and social development. This is proven by the fact that India and America both enjoy the same level of democracy as Great Britain and France. It is democracy itself which will lead us to a political, social, academic and economic revival.

Let us now deal briefly with the various arguments that speak against an immediate and full implementation of democracy.

The idea that political stability and security can only grow on the basis of a free democratic system is quite true. It is only possible for a government to change orderly and peacefully when it has the confidence of the majority. This is one of the basic conditions for economic development. In such a system representation can be easily changed and there is no reason for anger or resentment. The satisfaction that is part of such a system is a real and a deep-rooted one. It creates the right environment and atmosphere for quick economic development.

It is also true that development progress is impossible without the consent and participation of a majority of the people. This consensus cannot come about without letting the people participate in the decision-making process. This, in turn, requires freedom of political expression.

Fortunately, Yemen is one of the few countries in the world that is free from ethnic and religious conflicts. All of us believe in the same religious creed, Islam, and we all belong to one ethic group: the community of the Arabs.

Only our tribal structure bears some potential for conflict. Yet despite its negative impacts, tribalism has never been an obstacle for the development of democracy. It will only become a problem if certain parties stir up the tribal feelings of past rivalries or regional differences. Our people have experienced the peaceful transfer of power more than once without interference from tribal segments. Actually our tribal society is more suited for democratic development than those societies based on feudalism or serfdom prevalent in Europe before the establishment of democracy.

Many African researchers and some Western authors maintain that tribal roots actually stimulate the establishment of a modern democratic system. Traditional societies attach a lot of importance to dialogue, respecting the other view even if it opposes one's own. They are keen on taking decisions that are supported by a majority. Some Western writers have echoed the view that tribal structure is constructive to the establishment of modern democracy. One author, for example, discovered that there existed a kind of constitution to which tribes refer. - Another woman writer from the West opposes the idea that Great Britain brought democracy from the West to Africa. Instead, she argues, exactly the opposite took place. British colonialism attempted to erase many of the national and indigenous forms of democracy that were present in those societies.[1]

We, the people of Yemen, have all been reared within the frame of a tribal society. We can safely state that our tribal system has a higher level of sophistication since it has adopted customs, traditions and patterns of behavior from the religion of Islam, and from former highly developed civilizations.

Guarantees for Democracy in Yemen

Only the full and exact application of the democratic system is a real guarantee for the continuation of democracy. Democracy, according to a description by Abraham Lincoln, is "a system that, like a bundle of wooden sticks, is tossed about on stormy waters, always getting wet but never sinking". Under the democratic system people can express their views and interests in various peaceful ways, be it through the newspapers or other media. Democracy gives a feeling of political stability and security that is very conductive to economic development. It is in the wake of despotism that weapons are carried for self-defense and widespread corruption prevails, ultimately leading to a halt of development. Within the democratic system, however, social institutions expand and grow deep roots, cherishing the values of freedom. The distinction between the governing and the governed decreases and so does the competition for reaching those governing positions. It also leads to a peaceful transition of power. In the atmosphere of democracy regional differences shrink, since they usually have their historic roots in injustice and discrimination. Democracy also increases popular control over government agencies, and places restrictions and regulations upon them in order to prevent the misuse of public funds or the allocation of these funds by the ruling party. Public awareness about political rights increases, which in turn becomes an effective protection of the democratic system.

In our specific Yemeni situation, we may be able to come up with some more guarantees for safeguarding our democracy. High morality, truthfulness, justice, equality and altruism are all values inherent in our Islamic religion. We are capable of nurturing the spirit of freedom and patriotism, because these principles are already present in the tribal structure of our society. We will be able to establish a sound legal and constitutional system. The judiciary will be strengthened and its independence and purity guaranteed. All those civil and military institutions that are still divided can be united.

It seems that much of the fear that surrounds the unrestricted establishment of democracy comes from the great amount of power that will be given to parliament. According to article 82 of our constitution, the political party wining a majority in the council of deputies is given the right to form the new government. Not only this, but it will also be able to form the presidency of the republic. The text of the article states that the highest political authority of the republic is given to the Presidential Council, which consists of five members elected by the Council of Deputies. The winning party, according to those critical voices, is indeed the power to change the civil servants on all levels in military and civil institutions and can even change the laws themselves, giving the entire republic a new direction.

In order to overcome this dilemma, it is proposed to change articles 82 and 83 of the constitution and let the President of the Republic be elected by the people directly in free elections. In that way, all important political decisions, whether they concern laws, the ratification of treaties, the appointment of civil or military officials. the creation of authorities and corporations or their dissolution, must win the approval of the President and the cabinet. The direct election of the President by the people will create a positive balance between Parliament and the Presidency that will have a positive effect on the decision-making process. Finally, the government itself should be decentralized and power distributed to the local councils, enabling these freely elected bodies to fulfill their duties and responsibilities.

---

[1] Dr. Mohamed Mahmoud Rabia, Revolutionary Theory and Problems of Democracy in the Third World, Tripoli, Dar Maktabat al Fikr, 1974, pages 19 and 21.

Epiloque

The 1993 Parliamentary Elections in Yemen

by Fritz Piepenburg

Democracy in Yemen as a concept of public participation in governmental affairs is by no means confined to the two republics, the former Yemen Arab Republic (YAR) in the North, and the former People's Democratic Republic (PDRY) in the South. The legendary Queen of Sheba was widely believed to have ruled her kingdom heavily relying on the help of a council of elders and wise men. For thousands of years, the tribesmen of the northern part of Yemen have convened in large assemblies in order to select one leader from their midst: the *sheikh* of the tribe or - on the next higher level - the *sheikh* of the tribal federation. Even on the level of the village the *sheikh* was elected (which simply means agreed upon) by the male adult members of the location, to whom he was responsible and by whom he could be removed if his conduct as a leader became unacceptable.[1]

The sultans in the southern part did not begin as hereditary family dynasties of petty south Arabian states. This final stage in the development of the sultanates was rather the result of British colonial policies.[2] Originally, the sultans were elected by the *sheikhs* of several tribal units to act as their mediator or coordinator.

Islam throughout its 1400 years of existence has known a religious form of democracy, called the *shura* council or the council of the *ulama* (council of the learned men of religion). Many Muslim scholars regard *shura* (consultation) as one of the main pillars of the *shari'a* (Islamic legislation).[3] In verse 38 of sura XLII the believers are characterized as "those who conduct their affairs by mutual consultation". This famous verse was taken as motto by many parliaments in the Islamic world, including the Yemeni parliament.

Such forms of democracy, of course, do not originate from the developments of the European renaissance and enlightenment. They are much older than that. Unfortunately, even some Arab commentators tend to equalize the word "democracy" with the definition of the term brought about by Western Europe during the 17th and 18th centuries. Modern parliamentary democracy arguably might be the most broad and advanced form of public participation in the affairs of the government, but it is by no means the only one.

Setting the Stage

The compilation of the Holy National Charter in 1948 by the movement of the Free Yemenis ought to be considered the earliest attempt in Yemen to establish a government of public participation according to our modern understanding of democracy. The Charter was to become the foundation for a constitutional monarchy, which was to replace the absolute regime of Imam Yahia. Abdullah al-Wazir, the newly proclaimed Imam of Yemen after the assassination of Imam Yahia, was part of the Free Yemenis and fully agreed to the text of the Charter. The Charter foresaw the convention of a national assembly, which should decide on a future constitution. The division of power was envisioned, as well as the establishment of a freely and publicly elected *shura* council (parliament).[4] All those efforts came to a sudden end when crown prince Ahmad successfully incited tribesmen of the Hajjah area to overrun and sack Sana'a. Abdullah al-Wazir and those members of the movement of the Free Yemenis unfortunate enough to be present in the city were all killed. The socio-political development of North Yemen was thrown back for decades.

South Yemen during the pre-republican years also witnessed attempts of introducing ways of modern democracy. Two examples are most outstanding and worth mentioning here. As early as in 1952, a constitution was compiled for the sultanate of Lahij. The sultan himself was to appoint the 21 members of the legislative council, which was to take office for a period of two years. During this initial phase, the people of Lahij were to be made familiar with the idea of electing their own representatives for the next legislative period. The 21 members of the council represented all strata of society. Female deputies were representing the women of the sultanate, a highly progressive step for that early time.

The other example of installing a constitution and establishing a legislative council comes from the small state of Dathinah, north east of Aden. The constitution was drafted in 1961. The legislative council was to represent all levels of society and select a president from among their midst. The president of the council would also hold the position of the president of state, with powers over the executive and a great deal of influence over the jurisdiction as well. The position of the president would follow a system of rotation, allowing each council member to rise to the presidency for a limited period of time.[5]

The British, in an attempt to give greater stability to their colonial rule, established a legislative council in Aden in 1947 as an advisory body to the British governor. All members were appointed by the government itself. In 1959, the first full elections to the legislative council were held. Voters and candidates were submitted to highly restrictive conditions, such as stringent property and residence requirements. Out of a population of 180,000 only 21,554 were deemed eligible voters and, in protest of those restrictions, only 5600 votes were actually cast.[6]

Earlier, in 1954, the British prepared a constitution for the Federation of South Arabia. Robin Bidwell, who served as a political officer in the Western protectorates between 1955 and 1959, described it as "a constitution, while doubtless admirable from the point of view of a political scientist, which bore little resemblance to the facts of life in Southern Arabia".[7] When it was finally revised by a constitutional conference it was already too late and could not cope with the fast-rising tide of Arab nationalism. In a last and desperate effort to reverse the direction of history, Richard Turnbull, the last of the Aden governors, suspended the constitution and placed the Federation under direct colonial rule. It was of little avail. By November 30, 1967 - much earlier than originally planned - the last political officer left Aden.

The period of the two republics, of course, witnessed numerous attempts to draft constitutions and form popular legislative bodies. Altogether eight different sets of elections laws were passed in Yemen, three in the former PDRY, and four in the former YAR. The eighth and final set of election laws took effect in 1992 for the unified Republic of Yemen, paving the way for the parliamentary elections on April 27, 1993.

Previously, two parliamentary elections had taken place in the North and in the South respectively. In the northern part, a *shura* council was elected in 1971, then suspended by the late President Ibrahim al-Hamdi, and later reinstated as an appointed constitutional assembly. In 1988, a new *shura* council was elected in a highly successful nationwide balloting.

In the former PDRY, the Supreme People's Council (the parliament) was elected in 1978, and then again in 1987. From the day of unification on May 22, 1990, these two parliaments from the North and from the South merged and formed a new legislative body for the transitional period of united Yemen. The transitional period was to end by nationwide election of a new parliament, which in turn would elect the new president of the republic.

The Political Landscape after Unification

It is true, that the institution of a multi-party system in Yemen came as a direct result of the national reunification. Now, for the first time, Yemen was headed by two, not just one political organization: the People's General Congress (PGC) - the governing party of the former YAR - and the Yemen Socialist Party (YSP) - the governing party of the former PDRY. An immediate merger of the two parties was out of the question. With two parties clearly established in the political landscape of Yemen, the right for other parties to exist could no longer be denied. The way was finally cleared for other parties to emerge from their previous underground existence, or to be formed as entirely new entities.

After issuing the party and political organization law in October of 1991, the political soil of Yemen began mushrooming with new parties. At least 46 parties were registered in the span of only one year after passing the law. Out of this number, 21 parties came up with their own candidates for the new parliamentary elections, and 14 parties presented written election programs.[8] Ten parties were considered important enough to have their representatives included in the Supreme Election Committee (SEC). These ten parties deserve to be analyzed a bit further. Eight of them finally succeeded in having one or more of their representatives elected into the new parliament.

The People's General Congress (PGC) (al-mu'tamar ash-sha'bi al-am)

The PGC was originally formed in the early 80ies as a national political organization, under whose umbrella people of various political inclination could meet and discuss ideas, eventually overcoming their differences and acting jointly. Since the organization was formed by President Saleh and his political advisors, it inevitably adopted his political outlook from its very inception. A powerful network of governors, high administrative officials and even men of the jurisdiction was created all over the former YAR. The architects of the PGC did not so much insist on being faithful to a certain party line or doctrine (which did not even exist), as skillfully support popular persons of high standing among the local community. This policy paid off in the last two parliamentary elections, when the PGC both times won a clear majority of votes. Victory did not come because of the party's popularity with the people in the countryside, but because of the popularity of the candidate nominated by the party.

Before the first actual congress convened in 1982, an appointed committee drafted the National Charter, which was to function as a national political paper of consensus accepted by all politically active people (including representatives from long established but forbidden political parties). Once the political landscape changed and other parties were allowed to operate openly, it became clear that the PGC was actually President Saleh's party and the National Charter a rather generally formulated party program. By then, however, the PGC had created a sufficiently broad base at the grassroots level not to feel threatened any more by the other, much older parties of the North.

The Yemen Socialist Party (YSP)
(al-hizb al-ishtiraki al-yamani)

The Yemen Socialist Party was officially founded in 1978 in the former PDRY as a Marxist-Leninist political organization styled after the communist party of the former Soviet Union. And like its mentor in the former USSR, the YSP put great emphasis on sophisticated means of political organization and party discipline. The party draws its strength from a base of firmly committed members, much more so than from the one man on the top. Many of the activists of the YSP have received training in the former Soviet Union and display a remarkable ability to organize people politically by using modern propaganda tools - a fact that became clear even after unification in May 1990 during the transitional period.

The YSP was quick to react to the breath-taking developments in Eastern Europe beginning in the late 80ies. The party quickly announced a change of politics, even to the point of allowing the free establishment of other parties one year before national unification. Doubts remain, however, on how much that change of politics represents a change of heart. The core membership of the YSP, of course, remains the same before and after the end of the cold war. The new direction after abandoning its original Marxist principles is far from clear. The process of redefining aims and restructuring its internal organization continues.

The Islah Party (at-tajammu al-yamani lil-islah)

The *Islah* Party (literal translation: the Yemeni Congregation for Reform) is a newcomer to the political scene of Yemen. During its very short span of life, it grew to the most popular Islamist party.[9] *Islah*, of course, did not just appear out of nowhere, but was formed by merging various long-standing Islamist organizations, such as the Muslim Brotherhood (founded in Egypt in 1928 by Hasan al-Bana) and the Wahhabi movement (a strictly puritanical interpretation of Islam originating in Saudi Arabia).

Several factors rocketed *Islah* into the highest possible orbit of Yemen's political life, putting it on equal footing with the two ruling parties, the PGC of the former North and the YSP of the former South. Firstly, *Islah* succeeded in making maximum use of the current rising popular demand for original, pure and unadulterated religious values. In its main message to the people, *Islah* suggests that it is the only political organization which represents the true values of Islam. It is only through *Islah* that the various ailments of the country can receive a lasting cure. Secondly, it inherited a vast and highly effective network of mosques and religious institutions (al-ma'ahit al-'ilmiyah), which gave its politics instant access to the grassroots level. Thirdly, it received a major ally in Sheikh Abdullah al-

Ahmar, who came to regard *Islah* as the only viable alternative to the two established parties, the PGC and the YSP. He brought with him, as a wedding gift so to say, the tribal loyalty of the entire Hashid confederation, whose leader he is.

Naturally, this wide coalition of various Islamist and tribal groupings bears the potential of inter-party disagreements and even schisms.[10] So far, the alliance appears to hold well, and Sheikh Abdullah al-Ahmar remains the undisputed head of *Islah*.

Among the various groupings that make up *Islah*, the puritanical Wahhabi movement is probably the least democratic element among the party. An analysis conducted by the Washington based International Republican Institute in January 1993 foresees the "abrogation of the democratic system and severe restrictions on individual rights", if this wing should ever gain sufficient political power.[11] A highly informative piece of paper, in this regard, is the final resolution of the Conference for Peace and Unity, engineered by Abdulmajid az-Zindani between December 27 and 30, 1992. Az-Zindani has his ideological roots in the Muslim Brotherhood, but more recently has been advocating views and goals typical for the Wahhabi movement. The resolution of the above mentioned conference demands the establishment of a religious police force to control the "conduct and behavior of the people". It also foresees a highly restrictive role to be played by the female side of society in public life.[12] The ultimate goal is the establishment of a dawlah Islamiyah, an "Islamic state" with a narrowly and arbitrarily interpreted *shari'ah* as the exclusive source for all legislation.

The Ba'th parties (hizb al-ba'th al-'arabi al-ishtiraki)

There are in fact three wings of the party working in Yemen: the biggest and most influential is the Iraqi *Ba'th*; the much smaller Syrian *Ba'th*; and a Yemeni *Ba'th* which can be described as an attempt to create a Yemeni version of the Iraqi *Ba'th*. Like the Nasserites, the Bathists have a long-standing tradition of influential friendship with the political leadership of Yemen in general and the military in particular. President Ali Abdullah Saleh and his close associates reportedly come from a Bathist background before establishing their own political organization in the form of the PGC. A close connection between the Iraqi *Bath* and the PGC exists till the present day. The Bathist influence upon Yemen's stand in the Gulf crisis can hardly be overestimated.

The Nasserite parties (al-ahzab an-nasiriyah)

Three separate Nasserite parties were represented in the Supreme Election Committee. The largest one is the Nasserite Popular Unification Organization (NPUO) (at-tanzim al-wahadawi an-nasiri), which claims to be the original Nasserite party and heir of the political thought of Jamal Abdulnasser (the late Egyptian president of the 1950s). The organization also maintains that the two others, namely the Democratic Nasserite Party (DNP) (al-hizb an-nasiri ad-dimuqrati) and the Nasserite Popular Correction Organization (NPCO) (tanzim at-tashih ash-sha'bi an-nasiri) were merely the creations of the PGC and the YSP respectively to counteract its activities.

The Nasserites were very popular during the years of the civil war and for most of the 70s. Abdullah as-Sallal, leader of the 26th September Revolution, was an ardent admirer of Jamal Abdulnasser. The late President Ibrahim al-Hamdi very much favored the Nasserite party to the point of alienating politicians and army officials from other parties.

The Haqq Party (hizb al-haqq)

Haqq (the Party of Truth) could be called the second most popular Islamist Party. Until now, however, it is dwarfed by the much larger *Islah*, as it was recently proved during the parliamentary elections. Nevertheless, many people, including leading members of *Islah* themselves, regard this rather small party the only immediate challenge to the much larger *Islah*. Both parties, in the word of one political observer, "fight with the same sword". Both are Islamist parties with a claim to follow the best (meaning the exclusive best) interpretation of the Holy Quran and the Traditions of the Prophet Muhammad. The deep roots of *Haqq* in the Zaidi school of Islam are both its strength and its weakness: strength, because - unlike *Islah* - *Haqq* can claim to be of purely Yemeni origin, building on a Yemeni tradition that goes back to the 9th century AD; weakness, because it is exactly this tradition which gives it popularity only in the northern governorates of Sadah, Hajjah and maybe Sana'a. The future growth or stagnation of *Haqq* will largely depend on how well the party leadership succeeds in making the party a truly populist organization able to attract votes not only from the Zaidi north, but from the much larger Shafi'i south as well.

The League of the Sons of Yemen (Rabitah)
(hizb rabitat abna al-Yaman)

Rabitah is the oldest nationalist political party in Yemen, whose origin goes back to the year 1950, when British occupation of South Yemen was still an unchallenged fact. Originally named the "League of the Sons of South Arabia", the party's goal was to unify the petty South Arabian states into one united and independent South Arabia. After independence, the League, like other moderate South Yemeni political organizations, was forced into exile, from where it returned to Yemen only at the time of national unification. Only then it changed its name to "League of the Sons of Yemen" and acquired the profile of an outspoken party whose voice could not be ignored. The League is one of the most fearless critics of the faults and shortcomings of the ruling parties. It took the initiative in uniting five smaller parties into a national opposition block after the 1993 parliamentary elections.

Federation of Popular Yemeni Forces (FPYF)
(ittihat al-quwa ash-sha'biyah al-yamaniyah)

The Federation is another historically based party centering around the al-Wazir family. The most prominent representative was the short-lived Imam Abdullah al-Wazir in 1948. Other prominent members of the family are based in the United States of America. The party advocates a blend of Socialism and Islamism and appears to still draw much of its inspiration from the Iranian Islamic revolution. Its popular support depends to a large extent on areas with traditional influence by the al-Wazir family.

The Supreme Election Committee

One of the most important factors determining success or failure of the electoral process, from a technical as well as a political viewpoint, was the composition of the Supreme Election Committee (SEC). According to the Election Law8 passed on June 8, 1992 by the Presidential Council, the SEC consists of a president, vice president and a minimum of five committee members. According to the Law,[13] members to the SEC are appointed by the Presidential Council from among 50 candidates proposed by the Council of Deputies (the parliament). The Law also allows the Presidential Council to appoint additional members from the list of candidates, if need should arise. And it apparently arose, as shall be seen later.

The SEC is given all authority and independence in interpreting the Election Law and running the elections. It can only work properly, if its membership is accepted and acknowledged by all major political parties, which will be keen on having their representatives participating. A total of 17 members were appointed by political decree,[14] representing the 8 main parties plus a number of independent members. The only female member, Raqiyah Humaydan, was originally proposed by the YSP, but finally entered the SEC as an independent against the will of the Islamist parties. She is also the first woman-lawyer in Yemen and has a reputation of excellence and integrity.

The SEC's first task was to elect from among its members a president and a vice president. Abdulkarim Abdullah Al-Arashi (PGC) was chosen as president. Al-Arashi, who normally is being referred to as Qadi al-Arashi (qadi meaning religious judge) is a well experienced and widely respected politician. He first attracted international attention in 1978, when after the assassination of the late President Hussein al-Ghashmi, he headed the interim government until Ali Abdullah Saleh was elected new President by the Constituent Assembly. Al-Arashi continued to serve as the vice-president until national unification on May 22, 1991, when he became a member of the newly formed Presidential Council.

According to the first legal decision[15] agreed upon by the SEC, the president of the SEC holds the supreme authority of the Committee. He is not only chairing the numerous and long sessions of the SEC, but his signature is required for each paper to become legal and official, as well as for each check to become valid. Qadi al-Arashi is furthermore one of the few politicians who, by virtue of their personality and standing alone, and not only because of an assigned position, can defuse squabbles and differences among the members of the SEC before they reach a point of dangerous escalation. It was clear from the very first meeting of the SEC, of course, that its members would carry the political views and aspirations of their political parties right into the middle of the sessions, even though they had to officially resign from their parties. Qadi Abdulkarim al-Arashi is probably the one person who deserves most of the credit awarded to the SEC for succeeding in its difficult task of planning and running the entire election process.

Muhammad Sa'id Abdullah (YSP) was given the mandate of vice president of the SEC. Muhammad Abdullah is a well-known politician in the ranks of the YSP, holding the position of Minister of Housing in the former PDRY since May 1984. Before that, he headed the National Security Apparatus of the former PDRY, first as deputy minister of interior until May 1974, and then as minister of state security. Especially the latter position has earned him uncertain fame, notably because of his ways of dealing with political dissidents.[16]

According to Regulation No.1 of the SEC, the vice president takes the president's chair during his absence, signing all legal papers and cheques issued by the SEC in place of him. His main task, however, is to assist the president in fulfilling his duties.

Because of its broad political basis, the SEC does represent a wide spectrum of old and new parties operating in Yemen. No party of any significance threatened at any point of the election process to boycott the ballot, which could have had disastrous consequence. Instead, technical and even political differences were sorted out among the members of the SEC before exploding into open and public confrontation.

Another early step taken by the SEC was the formation of six sub-committees and the definition of their duties and responsibilities. The technical committee worked on the actual implementation of the various decisions; the legal committee made sure every step taken by the SEC was in accordance with the constitution and the Islamic laws; the public relations committee acted as the SEC spokesman and regulated issues of campaigning; the security committee dealt with the safety of voters and candidates; the financial committee was responsible for the budget; and the secretarial committee did all of the administrative work.

Choosing the Constituencies

Deciding on the exact boundaries of the constituencies was, in the words of Sadiq Amin Abu Ras, head of the technical committee[17], "one of the most difficult tasks during the preparatory phase, taking several months." Each constituency was to accommodate an average number of 49,732 inhabitants, allowing for a variation of plus or minus 5%. This figure was derived from the population-census-estimate of December 1992, which puts the total number of the republic's inhabitants at 14,256,724 (a figure, which includes Yemeni emigrants living abroad).

Care was taken not to allow constituencies overlap borders of the governorates. As much as possible, the borders of the constituency were drawn identical with the borders of the directorates (the next administrative level below the governorate). If the directorate was too big, it was divided taking demographic, geographic, administrative and social aspects into consideration. Traditional tribal borders were a highly sensitive point and needed careful consideration, if the SEC wanted to make sure that a maximum number of voters would turn up and cast their ballots in peace. Detailed maps of each province, directorate and larger city were compiled, indicating the exact boundaries of the constituencies.

Finally, 301 constituencies were formed with almost identical numbers of inhabitants. Only Al-Mahra was an exception, which was divided into two constituencies with populations exceeding the number originally envisioned.

Table 1: Constituencies and Election Centers

Nr.	Governorat	No. of Constituencie	No. of Election Centers
1	Sanaa city	18	84
2	Aden	11	73
3	Taiz	43	227
4	Lahij	12	100
5	Ibb	38	227
6	Abian	8	88
7	Al-Baidha	10	79
8	Shabwah	6	84
9	Hadhramawt	17	170
10	Al-Mahrah	2	30
11	Al-Hudaydah	34	175
12	Dhamar	21	150
13	Sanaa	9	50
14	Al-Mahwit	36	227
15	Hajjah	8	47
16	Sa'dah	23	147
17	Al-Jawf	2	20
18	Marib	3	39
	Total	301	2017

There were proposals to add the island of Socotra to Al-Mahra and then create a third constituency. But finally it was decided that Socotra should remain with Aden, thus keeping the province in one piece. All other constituencies consisted of the target figure of 47,365 give or take 5%. The fact that the SEC succeeded in dividing the whole country so equally into 301 constituencies "surpassed our previous expectations" (Final Report) and appeared like a good omen foreshadowing a successful balloting.

Next came the task of deciding on the various election centers within one constituency. Factors determining the choice of the center were the geographic proximity, population density and availability of centrally located public buildings. Tribal structures and borders were again carefully taken into consideration to give each person an equal chance to cast the ballot. The SEC would only take a final decision on these matters after extensively consulting with government officials and popular leaders of any given area. A total of 2017 election centers were identified for the 301 constituencies. Each constituency had one main election center and several branch election centers (see Table 1).

This work of dividing the country into the constituencies and identifying the election centers took more than 3 months of hard work and can be considered a pioneer effort by the first SEC. All subsequent Sec's will have a much easier task and can refer to a wealth of previously completed work and experiences.

The Registration of Voters

Each election center needed a staff, forming the Committee for the Registration of Voters. The Registration Committee was to update the previously compiled name list for each constituency, and properly register those inhabitants willing to participate in the balloting and fulfilling the basic qualifications (Yemeni nationality, above the age of 18, etc.). The staff was basically recruited from civil servants. A budget was given to each main election center and all expenses generously reimbursed. Before starting work, all members of the committees underwent three days of basic training taking place in the main cities. From there, each committee (consisting of one director and two assistants) would first contact the Supervising Committee located in the respective provincial capital to receive the necessary working materials. A total of 12,156 men and women were employed in the various election councils and spread out over an area of more than 500,000 km2.

Voters' registration started on January 21, 1993 and lasted for exactly 30 days. All throughout the 30 days, the SEC was extremely busy dealing with different problems and inquiries from the various registration committees. The official newspapers were filled each day with reports on the progress of the registration. Members of the SEC would address the public mainly through television and give clarification on certain issues. Sana'a Radio established a hotline, where anybody with a telephone could speak directly with a high official (usually a member of the Supervising Committee), while everybody else who had his radio set tuned in could listen to the conversation. Some people even started grumbling at the television. program. Instead of the usual soap opera after the 9 o'clock news, viewers were presented with more details on how to register their names properly day after day.

After closing registration, the committees prepared the updated namelists, which were then posted outside the main election centers for 7 days. The people of the constituencies could check, if their name was properly included, and bring mistakes to the attention of the members.

A total of 2,661,323 people registered in all of Yemen, including 502,379 female voters (for more details see Table 2 and Charts 1, 2 and 3). On the male side, 70% of all eligible voters did register during the 30 day period. The female registration was much lower, as was expected, and reached only 16% of all eligible women voters. This low number of female registration is the main reason why the later ratio of actual voters (both men and women) to eligible voters reached only 36%.

Chart 1 gives an overview of registered voters compared with eligible voters in absolute numbers. Naturally, those provinces with a high population will come first, while the more sparsely populated provinces come last.

Chart 2 tells something about political awareness in the various governorates,

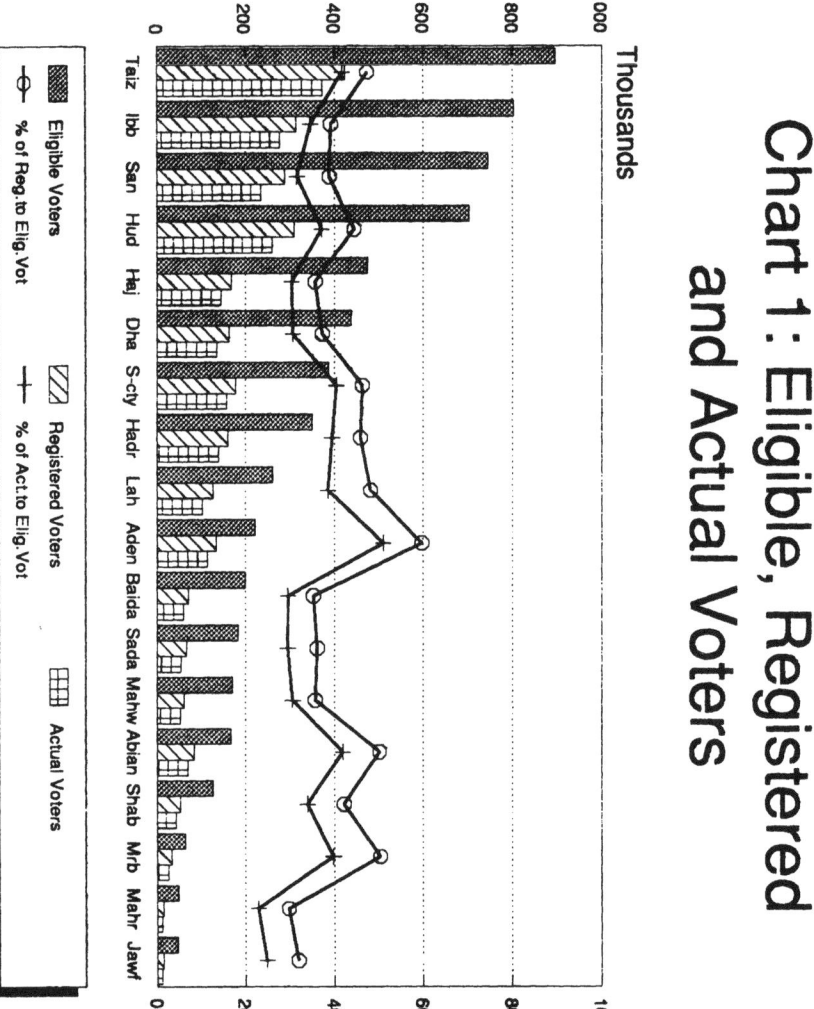

Chart 1: Eligible, Registered and Actual Voters

Table 2: Population and Voters per Governorate

Nr	Governorate	Total Population			Eligible Voters			Registered Voters			% of Registered to Eligible Voters			Actual Voters	% of Act. to Elig. Voters
		male	female	total	male	female	total	male	female	total	male	female	total		
1	Sanaa city	430,993	447,867	878,860	189,939	197,375	387,314	136,767	41,859	178,626	72%	21%	46%	156,408	40%
2	Aden	248,328	258,051	506,379	109,438	113,723	223,161	62,177	71,139	133,316	57%	63%	60%	113,610	51%
3	Taiz	995,108	1,034,069	2,029,177	438,544	455,714	894,258	325,881	96,092	421,973	74%	21%	47%	372,172	42%
4	Lahij	292,673	304,131	596,804	128,981	134,031	263,012	103,189	23,099	126,288	80%	17%	48%	101,300	39%
5	Ibb	894,364	929,379	1,823,743	394,146	409,578	803,724	271,572	42,910	314,482	69%	10%	39%	278,684	35%
6	Abian	185,536	192,800	378,336	81,765	84,967	166,732	61,791	21,632	83,423	76%	25%	50%	69,652	42%
7	Al-Baidha	223,576	232,330	455,906	98,530	102,388	200,918	59,676	11,310	70,986	61%	11%	35%	59,648	30%
8	Shabwah	139,291	144,745	284,036	61,386	63,789	125,175	39,024	13,639	52,663	64%	21%	42%	42,581	34%
9	Hadhramawt	389,970	405,237	795,207	171,860	178,588	350,448	103,095	57,204	160,299	60%	32%	46%	138,195	39%
10	Al-Mahrah	54,175	56,297	110,472	23,875	24,810	48,685	9,944	4,596	14,540	42%	19%	30%	11,190	23%
11	Al-Hudaydah	782,694	813,338	1,596,032	344,933	358,438	703,371	258,526	52,800	311,326	75%	15%	44%	261,125	37%
12	Dhamar	484,970	503,957	988,927	213,725	222,093	435,818	145,140	17,215	162,355	68%	8%	37%	134,041	31%
13	Sanaa	825,364	861,836	1,687,200	365,501	379,811	745,312	265,185	23,743	288,928	73%	6%	39%	236,241	32%
14	Al-Mahwit	188,007	195,367	383,374	77,759	91,194	168,953	57,332	3,064	60,396	74%	3%	36%	51,852	31%
15	Hajjah	526,264	546,868	1,073,132	231,924	241,005	472,929	153,432	15,310	168,742	66%	6%	36%	144,398	31%
16	Sa'dah	203,755	211,733	415,488	89,795	93,311	183,106	64,179	1,942	66,121	71%	2%	36%	54,210	30%
17	Al-Jawf	51,404	53,417	104,821	22,654	23,541	46,195	14,487	310	14,797	64%	1%	32%	11,533	25%
18	Marib	71,027	73,807	144,834	31,301	32,527	63,828	27,547	4,515	32,062	88%	14%	50%	25,344	40%
	Total	6,987,499	7,265,229	14,252,728	3,076,056	3,206,883	6,282,939	2,158,94	502,379	2,661,323	70%	16%	42%	2,262,18	36%

Chart 2: Percentage of Registered Voters compared with Eligible Voters

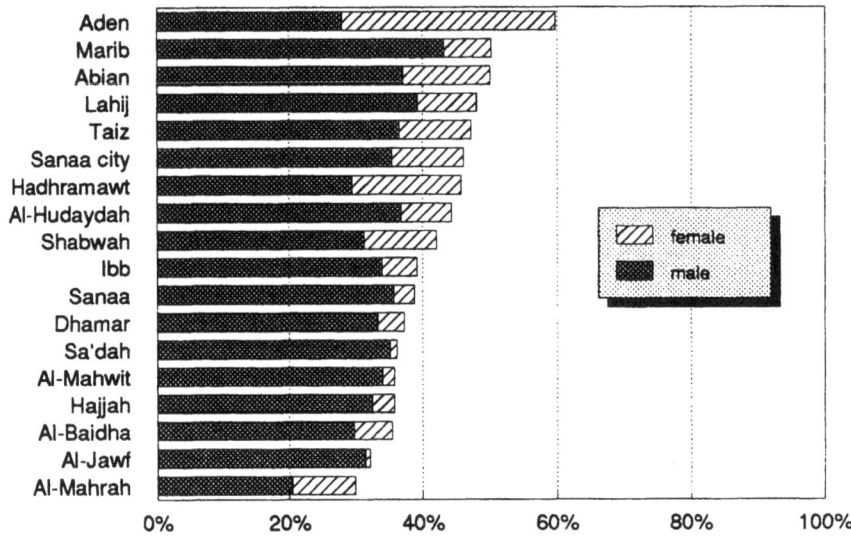

including female participation. Aden has the highest percentage of registered voters and the largest percentage of female registrations. In fact, Aden is the only province, where female registrations even outnumbered male registrations.

Aden is followed by the southern provinces of Abyan, Lahij, Taiz and Sana'a city. There is no surprise in this sequence. However, the Marib province taking second place after Aden does cause some eyebrows to rise. Why should Marib be so different from its neighboring provinces, such as Al-Jawf in the north and Al-Baidah in the south, both coming at the very end of the list? Some political observers speculate that the relatively high number of registered voters was achieved by the registration of large numbers of military personnel stationed in this province. And just for clarification: this practice is completely legal. According to the law, anybody can register in a certain district, if he fulfills one of three conditions: the area mapped out for the center includes his place of birth, or his place of residence, or his place of work.

Chart 3: Percentage of Actual Voters compared with Eligible Voters

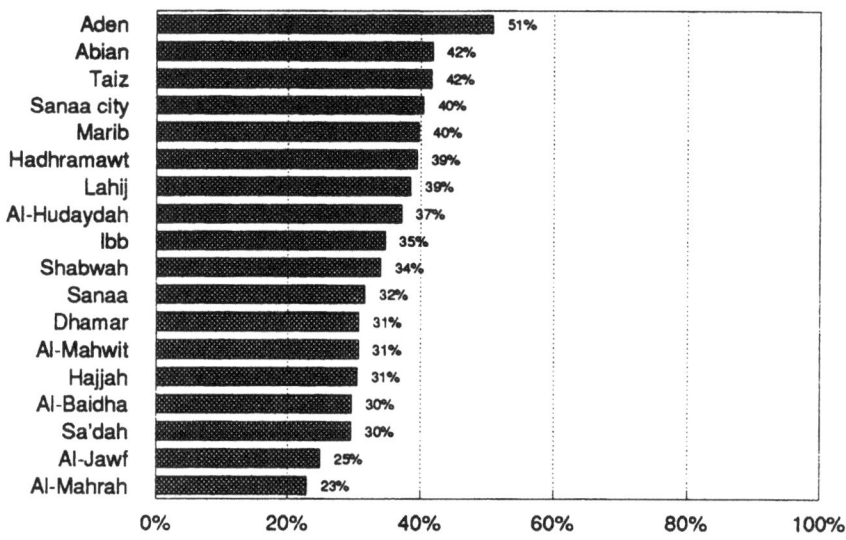

Registration of Candidates

Only one committee for the registration of candidates was established for each constituency, totaling 301 committees nationwide. The Technical Department of the SEC chose the committee members by lot and they appointed one as chairman. The new supervising committees on the governorate level were chosen the same way. After receiving training, the newly formed committees would leave for their assigned centers.

Registration of candidates started on March 28 and lasted for exactly 10 days. A total of 4,819 persons registered as candidates and all but nine were given a certificate of acceptance by the Technical Department of the SEC. Out of this number, 1,629 withdrew their candidacy, reducing the final number to 3,181 candidates. Only 41 of the total candidates were female, which amounts to less than 1.3%.

A total of 22 parties entered the race through their own candidates, some running in one electorate only. The PGC put up the largest number of candidates in 275 constituencies (only 1 candidate per constituency), followed by the YSP with 209 and the *Islah* with 187 candidates. With a surprisingly large number of 156 candidates, the *Ba'th* Party took place 4, followed by the *Rabitat Abna Al-Yaman* with 87 candidates. And then, of course, there were many independents (although some were not independent at all, as shall be seen later), totaling 1,968 candidates. The independents, of course, were not limited to one per constituency and could register themselves in unlimited numbers.

Concerning the female candidates, the PGC came up with a disappointing low figure of only two women candidates. The YSP had a total of four, but was also supporting independent female candidates in certain constituencies by not putting up an candidate of their own. *Ba'th* had two female candidates and the three Nasserite Parties one each. *Rabitah* came up with three ladies. 17 women entered the elections as independents. *Islah* and other Islamist parties, as was expected, did not come up with even one female candidate.

Campaigning followed an orderly way. Previously, the SEC had issued a whole set of regulations of proper and fair conduct in campaigning. It was forbidden to slander other candidates or entire parties. The use of loudspeakers was forbidden, except in specially approved rallies. According to regulation, only two posters of the same candidate were allowed to be posted side by side, and then only, if sufficient space was available. It was unlawful to tear down or post over already existing posters. Printing shops of all sizes, regardless, if they were equipped with the most sophisticated Heidelberg speedmaster or with a simple second-hand copy machine were busy day and night in preparing the posters, leaflets, handouts and party programs for the 3,181 candidates. While the larger parties followed a certain line in their campaigning, the independents were completely on their own. They were only aided by their immediate family members, who would do distribution and posting services. It was not an uncommon sight to see the old man himself gracefully and in his best clothes climbing up a ladder and gluing his own picture to the wall!

The SEC also granted parties and political organizations the right to use the official news media. In order to enjoy this privilege, the party had to prove that at least 15 of its members had registered themselves in 15 different constituencies as candidates. The 15 minutes or so given to each party on television became a highly popular program, watched by millions after the evening news. Spectators were shocked, how frankly some of the new parties criticized the shortcomings of the government and battered against corruption and mismanagement. Never before was it possible to hear such words on Yemen television since it first began to broadcast in September 1975.

Table 3: Winning Candidates

Nr.	Governorate	Nr. of Constituencies	PGC	YSP	Islah	Ba'th	Nasserites			Haqq	Independents
							NPU	DNP	NPCO		
1	Sanaa city	18	11	0	6	0	0	0	0	0	1
2	Aden	11	0	8	0	0	0	0	0	0	3
3	Taiz	43	8	6	18	1	1	1	0	0	8
4	Lahij	12	0	8	0	0	0	0	0	0	4
5	Ibb	38	17	2	13	0	0	0	0	0	6
6	Abian	8	1	7	0	0	0	0	0	0	0
7	Al-Baidha	10	2	3	2	1	0	0	0	0	2
8	Shabwah	6	1	5	0	0	0	0	0	0	0
9	Hadhramawt	17	1	11	0	0	0	0	0	0	5
10	Al-Mahrah	2	0	2	0	0	0	0	0	0	0
11	Al-Hudaydah	34	23	1	5	0	0	0	0	0	5
12	Dhamar	21	11	1	7	0	0	0	0	0	2
13	Sanaa	36	21	1	5	3	0	0	1	0	5
14	Al-Mahwit	8	5	0	0	0	0	0	0	0	3
15	Hajjah	23	15	0	3	2	0	0	0	0	3
16	Sa'dah	9	5	0	1	0	0	0	0	2	1
17	Al-Jawf	2	1	0	1	0	0	0	0	0	0
18	Marib	3	1	1	1	0	0	0	0	0	0
	Total	301	123	56	62	7	1	1	1	2	48
	% of total	100.0%	40.9%	18.6%	20.6%	2.3%	0.3%	0.3%	0.3%	0.7%	15.9%

NPUO: Nasserite Popular Unification Organisation
DNP: Democratic Nasserite Party
NPCO: Nasserite Popular Correction Organization

The Day of Balloting

For the third time it was the task of the SEC to form a sufficient number of polling committees and give them initial training. Polling committees were formed according to the list of registered voters, with the goal of having one polling station for a maximum of 450 male voters. Female committees were also selected - one for approximately 100 registered female voters. Thus, besides the 301 main polling committees, 5,420 branch committees for male voters and 1,541 committees for female voters were formed, staffed by a total of 21,786 men and women.

The immediate preparations began 3 days before the balloting, scheduled to take place on April 27th, 1993. Security precautions were given special consideration. In the capital Sana'a alone, more than 30,000 troops were employed, strictly controlling the main roads to Sana'a for arms smuggling and guarding the polling stations day and night. It almost felt like an invasion, when the soldiers moved in and jumped off their trucks, gun in one hand and rolled up mattress in the other, swarming about schools and other public buildings designated as polling stations. All over the republic, over 120,000 soldiers and security forces were put on duty. There were fears that extremists would attempt to disrupt the elections by bombing selected polling stations, eventually rendering the entire elections invalid. Fortunately, with the exception of one or two minor incidents, the election day passed by quietly and peacefully.

Meanwhile, over 300 journalists, correspondents and foreign observers had taken up their posts mainly in Sana'a. The SEC had established a highly effective information center at the Officers' Club, providing telephone lines, telex, picture transmission and constant updates of the latest news. The center also organized press conferences where political parties and individuals could publicly voice their opinions.

From the early morning at 8 o'clock, men and women frequented the various polling stations. Traffic decreased to a minimum, with most people preferring to walk rather than to drive. The peaceful gatherings in front of the polling stations were only temporarily disturbed when people lined up to watch a number of black limousines pulling up and driving right into the polling station. It was the President with some of his close aids, who visited all 18 stations in Sana'a and others in the surrounding villages. There was a widespread feeling of excitement and festivity.

Chart 4: Winning Candidates in all Constituencies

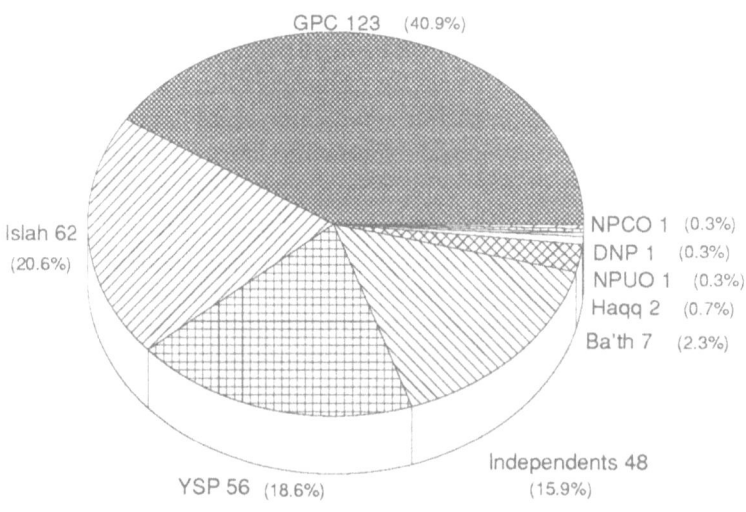

Total Seats: 301

Chart 5: Votes received by Parties and Independents

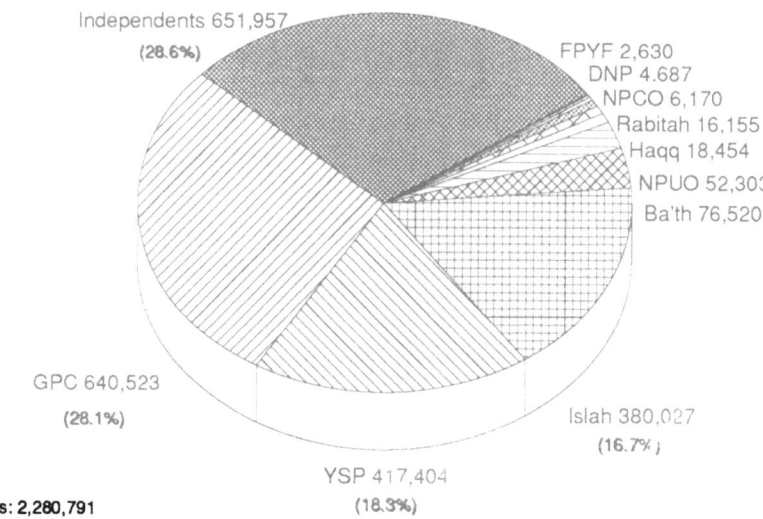

Total Votes: 2,280,791

The *haflat al-intikhabat*, the election festivity took hold of everyone. There was none of the moroseness which is common to election days in Europe. People enjoyed voting and they did it with a conviction as if they had done so many times before. 85% of all registered voters went to the polls that day. At 6 o'clock in the evening, the stations were closed - and the great day was over.

Results

Counting began immediately after the stations closed. In the presence of the candidates themselves or their designated representatives, the Balloting boxes at the branch polling stations were closed and sealed and then transported to the main station of the constituency. There, again in the presence of the candidates or their representatives, the boxes were opened one at a time and the counting began. By the evening of the next day, the first preliminary results were released by the SEC.

From the release of the very first figures it became clear that the PGC of President Saleh had taken an early lead. This did not come as a surprise. The real race, however, was for the second place between the YSP and the *Islah*. In the final

Table 4: Number of Votes attained by Parties and Independents

Nr.	Governorate	PGC	YSP	Islah	Ba'th	NPUO	DNP	NPCO	Haqq	Rabitah	FPYF	other parties	Independents
1	Sanaa city	61,892	24,760	36,762	1,698	2,692	12	165	2,085	865	134	732	33,737
2	Aden	7,183	47,679	6,401	508	768	351	150	0	524	0	2,512	47,534
3	Taiz	81,500	70,710	74,017	14,556	34,118	4,009	78	61	228	0	109	92,786
4	Lahij	3,959	54,480	147	339	1,518	0	0	0	629	0	545	39,683
5	Ibb	89,055	36,386	58,810	5,533	1,948	26	108	312	3,209	0	214	83,083
6	Ablan	13,280	37,504	3,164	0	1,129	0	0	0	349	55	264	13,928
7	Al-Baidha	14,659	16,571	10,826	3,881	1,399	2	0	423	270	83	1,154	14,463
8	Shabwah	8,738	18,398	2,206	291	0	0	0	0	2,636	84	84	10,228
9	Hadhramawt	20,433	45,605	22,930	342	48	0	0	12	2,788	0	113	45,924
10	Al-Mahrah	2,265	6,874	0	0	0	0	0	0	0	0	0	2,052
11	Al-Hudaydah	107,979	12,234	43,652	5,363	5,891	6	224	39	321	31	763	84,653
12	Dhamar	42,598	15,801	29,563	4,039	483	205	158	684	614	364	4,069	38,847
13	Sanaa	82,460	12,310	45,423	17,063	1,600	0	5,234	1,445	268	1,185	2,563	67,875
14	Al-Mahwit	21,612	1,054	7,751	2,921	0	0	53	33	86	0	0	18,342
15	Hajjah	53,158	8,335	29,544	13,301	250	76	0	210	3,322	235	324	34,856
16	Sa'dah	17,716	2,546	4,567	4,927	80	0	0	12,382	0	0	0	12,032
17	Al-Jawf	2,689	1,940	2,660	266	74	0	0	788	46	0	56	3,014
18	Marib	9,347	3,217	1,604	1,492	305	0	0	0	0	459	459	8,920
	Total	640,523	417,404	380,027	76,520	52,303	4,687	6,170	18,454	16,155	2,630	13,961	651,957
	% of total	28.1%	18.3%	16.7%	3.4%	2.3%	0.2%	0.3%	0.8%	0.7%	0.1%	0.6%	28.6%

NPUO: Nasserite Popular Unification Organisation
DNP: Democratic Nasserite Party
NPCO: Nasserite Popular Correction Organization
FPYF: Federation of Popular Yemeni Forces
Rabitah: League of the Sons of Yemen

Republic of Yemen - Parliamentary Elections 1993

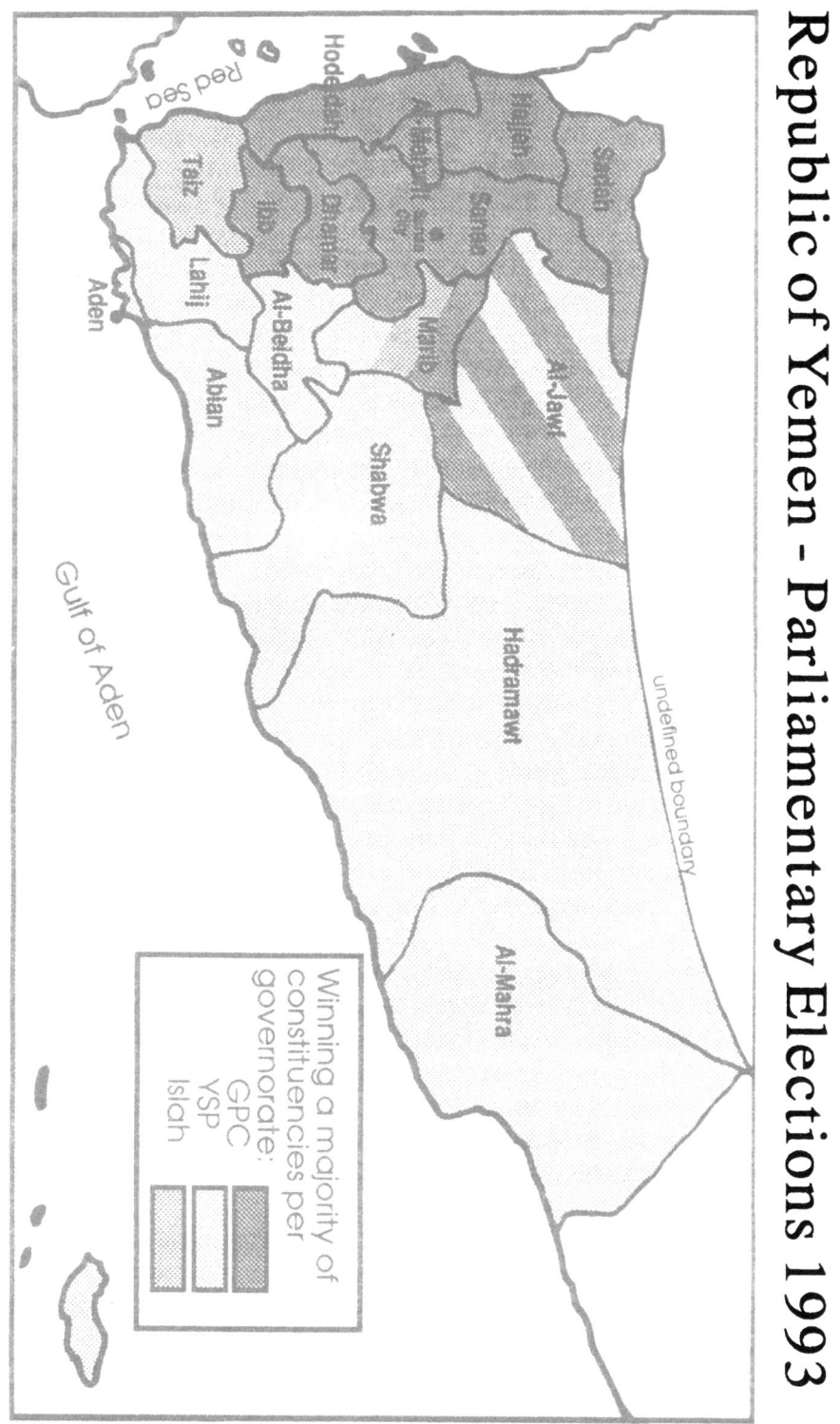

count, the PGC had won 122 out of the total number of 301 constituencies. *Islah* came in second with 62 constituencies and YSP third with 56 (the elections for one constituency in Hodeidah were delayed, therefore, the total number of elected representatives was only 300) (see Table 3 and Chart 4). The independents, too, did well, winning in 48 constituencies. Later on, 12 of the independent winners declared their true affiliation to be with the YSP, causing the Socialist to declare in one of their first press conferences after the elections to be the real second winner (with a total of 68 candidates in parliament).[18] The PGC was the first to react and claim that 14 of the independent winners were actually part of their party. *Islah* and other parties also voiced their claims upon the independents. The final report of the SEC correctly states that it cannot take these claims into consideration. Who ran as an independent won as an independent, even if he should later admit that he belongs to one of the parties.

Casting a look at the geographical distribution of the winning candidates, it becomes immediately evident that each of the two major parties had won a majority in the former provinces of North and South Yemen respectively (see Map "Republic of Yemen - Parliamentary Elections of 1993). *Islah*, the powerful newcomer, received its biggest support from the southern governorates of the former YAR, namely Dhamar, Ibb, and Taiz. *Islah*'s strongest performance was in the Taiz province, where it could take a clear majority of 18 constituencies, while the PGC and the YSP won only 8 and 6 respectively.

For the smaller parties, the election results turned out to be a big disappointment. Two of the parties represented in the SEC, namely *Rabitah* and FTYF, weren't able to win even one single seat in the parliament. The Nasserite parties could win only one seat for each of the three factions. The newly formed Islamist party *Haqq* won two constituencies (both in the Sadah governorate). Only the *Ba'th* Party could make some inroads with 7 of its candidates succeeding in their constituencies.

Only two female candidates succeeded in the elections. They are Khawlah Ahmad Sharaf from the YSP, who won in the Al-Mansurah constituency of the Aden province. Muna Salim Bashrahil won in her constituency in Mukalla, capital of the Province of Hadhramawt. She could succeed, because she received the full support of the YSP, which did not appoint an own candidate. A number of other female candidates came in second, such as Samiyah al-Ahmadi (PGC) in Rada', Tayyibah Muhammad Barakat (YSP) in Hodeidah, Radhiyah Shamshir (YSP) in Sanaa and Afrah ash-Shina (PGC) in Aden.

A glance at the number of actual voters gained by each party sheds a different light on the election result (see Table 4 and Chart 5).[19] According to the number of votes received, the YSP does take second place after the PGC, having obtained 18.3% of all votes cast. The *Islah* comes third with 16.7%. The largest number of votes (28.6%) was cast in favor of the independents; a fact that should send a message to the established parties. The PGC received a solid 28.1%.

The difference between votes cast for the *Ba'th* and for the NPUO, the main Nasserite party, accounts for just over 1%, indicating an equal level of popularity for the two long established political trends in Yemen. In winning actual seats in parliament, *Ba'th* got the much better deal with 7 candidates, compared with only 1 candidate by the NPUO. Again, the difference in the number of votes obtained by *Haqq* and *Rabitah* is only one tenth of a percent. Yet, *Haqq* won two seats, while *Rabitah* could not obtain a single one. The outcome of democratic elections, it seems, is not just a matter of receiving votes, but one of political luck as well.

Accusations of Fraud and Deception

Accusations of wrongdoing during the elections and the counting procedures surfaced almost immediately after the first results became known. The *Islah* was among the first to loudly protest perceived irregularities. On the fourth day after the elections, the party published as special edition of *as-Sahwa*[20] solely dedicated to the exposure of alleged election fraud. The huge headline read: "PGC and YSP share equally in the rigging of the elections". *Islah* especially deplored practices employed by the YSP, and even went so far as to threaten that it would not recognize the announced results in the southern and eastern provinces (those provinces identical with the former PDRY).

The PGC and the YSP immediately countered with accusations from their side against *Islah*. All the smaller parties and a good number of independents had some grievances over how the elections were handled. Accusations reached from "buying votes" to "smuggling pre-fabricated voting slips into the ballot boxes" or even "breaking the seals wantonly and changing its contents".[21] Before too long, over 70 appeals were filed with the Court of Appeals, prompting the Court to initially withhold some of the certificates to be handed out to the newly elected representatives.

One of the most incriminating statements came from Abdulmalik al-Mikhlafi after only 3 days of counting. Al-Mikhlafi, himself a member of the SEC and chairman of the Public Relations Committee (and therefore somebody to be taken seriously), accused the SEC and even the Court of Appeals of tacitly favoring the ruling parties[22]. President Saleh rejected all accusations of fraud as an attempt by unlucky parties and individuals to put the blame of their poor performance on somebody else. Eventually, most of the appeals were withdrawn, including the ones filed by *Islah*. Sheikh Abdullah al-Ahmar explained his party's withdrawal of most of the appeals in the following words: "The election was such a good experience ... that we should not scar the beautiful image with rejected and prolonged petitions and challenges".[23] The matter was, in other words, solved by political rather than juridical means. In fact, as soon as the final results were known, the leaders of the three winning parties, Ali Abdullah Saleh, Ali Salem Al-Beedh, and Sheikh Abdullah al-Ahmar, immediately met to work on a possible governing coalition. Elections were repeated in only three constituencies (No.252, 192, and 85 in Sana'a, Ibb and Hodeidah governorates). All other remaining accusations were solved on the political level.

Political observers point specifically to two areas of weakness which need to be solved before the next elections: The voting procedures for illiterates (it has been suggested to use icons and let the illiterate choose for himself, rather than through a third person); and the transportation of the sealed ballot boxes from the branch offices to the main polling station (where most of the serious attempts to rig the elections reportedly occurred).

Yet the overall evaluation of the 1993 parliamentary elections must lead to a positive result. Rarely did the nations of the Arab world, or even of the third world as a whole, see such well planned and smoothly conducted general parliamentary elections. Congratulations extended to Yemen by other countries, notably the United States and Western Europe, were heartfelt and sincere. Yemen, the small and perhaps not-so-significant country at the south-western rim of the Arabian Peninsula, had succeeded in winning the attention and even admiration of much bigger and more developed countries.

1 For more information on the tribal structure of the northern part of Yemen, see "Tribes, government and history in Yemen" by Paul K. Dresch, Oxford, 1989
2 This process is well explained in "PDR Yemen, Politics, Economics and Society" by Tareq Y. Ismail and Jaqueline S. Ismail, London 1984, pp. 9-11.
3 "The Spirit of Islam" by Afif A. Tabbara, Beirut 1988, pp. 292-294
4 For more information see "The Free Yemeni Movement 1935/1962" by J. Leigh Douglas, Beirut 1987
5 These two examples were taken from "Tatawwur an-nuzum al-intikhabi fi al-jumhuriya al-yamania" by Qa'id Muhammad Tarabush, Manshurat 26 September 1993
6 "PDR Yemen" p. 16
7 "The two Yemens" by Robin Bidwell, London 1983
8 For a useful comparison of election progress, see "Election Programs of Political Parties and Organizations in the Republic of Yemen" by Dr. Rashad M. al-Alimi and Dr. Ahmad A. al-Bishari, Sana'a 1993
9 It is incorrect to describe Islah as an Islamic party, since all parties in Yemen, without exception, adhere to Islam as their professed religion. "Islamist" implies the attempt to politicize Islam and employ religious sentiments for achieving political goals.
10 Sheikh Abdullah al-Ahmar confirmed that at least two major wings exist within Islah, an "ideological wing" and a "tribal wing", see Yemen Times Vol.2 No.24 p.3
11 "1993 National Elections in the Republic of Yemen" by International Republican Institute, Washington 1993
12 A translation of the final resolution has been published in the Yemen Times Vol.3 No.1 pp.7 and 11
13 Law No.41 of 1992
14 Presidential Decree No.4 of 1992, August 17, 1992
15 Regulation No.1 on the internal structure of the SEC
16 For more information see "PDR Yemen" p.67
17 "Final Report by the Technical Committee" by Sadiq Amin Abu Ras, Supreme Election Committee 1993
Note: All factual procedures on the election process, as well as all figures mentioned in this paper are taken from this report unless indicated otherwise.
18 Al-Hayat newspaper, No.11036
19 All number of actual votes are taken from: "Statistics on votes obtained by candidates of parties and political organizations" by the Technical Committee of the SEC
20 As-Sahwa newspaper No.366 of May 1st, 1993
21 An articulate view of an independent candidate who felt cheated by the bigger parties is given in the editorial of the Yemen Times, Vol.3 Is. 17, page 1
22 Al-Hayat newspaper No.11037 and Yemen Times Vol.3 Is.23 p.7
23 Yemen Times Vol.3, Is.23, p.9

Women and Democracy in Yemen

by Amat Al-Alim As-Suswa

It seems that the unbalanced evolution in male-female relationships in Arab countries including Yemen is a historic fact with cultural and economic roots deep within society[1]. It is also a fact that Arab societies have been heavily influenced by the international economic system ever since the rise of capitalism in America and Europe. This does not mean that there exists a cause-effect relationship. It merely indicates the existence of profound structural links between the two. Arab societies were exposed to a "culture shock" upon the sudden arrival of Western influence in the form of fleets first and administrative institutions later. It was precisely at the intersection between these two civilizations that the issues involved in women's liberation emerged[2].

Two Roads to Women's Emancipation in Yemen

The emancipation of women in Yemen has taken two different roads. During the colonial period and the early years after independence, the emancipation of women became an issue because of the need for overall development. It also developed, to a certain extent, as a result of the growing capitalistic relationships within the national economy. The conventional community structure was not in need of such emancipation.

South Yemen shared the experience of being subject to a foreign power with many other Arab countries. The struggle for the liberation of women was firmly embedded in the struggle for national independence.

Emancipation in southern Yemen must be viewed as part of defending Arab identity in Aden and the Protectorates. It was firmly tied to the struggle for preserving Arab heritage and deciding one's own destiny. Female participation in the fight for independence made the women's cause part of the higher cause of national liberation. When independence came, women found themselves facing new circumstances. They continued to reject all forms of subordination and demanded their rightful place in the society and at work. The South Yemeni situation was comparable to the situation in Egypt, Syria and Algeria, even though Algeria's youth, women's and labor movements had been associated with Islamic cultural values for reasons known to many.

In North Yemen after the 1962 revolution, the young republic did not have any strategy concerning women. The emancipation of women was looked at as a trivial issue. Yet, eventually, every problem would find a solution following the fall of the Imamate which resisted even the simplest attempts towards reform.

During the period prior to unification in the North, women's issues entered the political scene as part of the overall issue of development. This was quite different from the South Yemeni experience or that of other Arab countries having liberated themselves from foreign occupation. The politicians in power realized that without the liberation of women and their emancipation as full and equal members of society, all attempts to develop and modernize the country would be doomed to failure. Yet, at the same time, these politicians were clinging to what they perceived as "deep-rooted values and cultural structures", thus ultimately following a double standard.

Then, there has always been the deep rift between what was decided and announced and what was put into reality and practice. On the one hand, there were all those constitutional and legal promises, including international treaties on children's and women's rights. But their political application, on the other hand, looked quite different, as was the case with many other aspects of social evolution. One even gets the feeling that the academic elite of our Arab world is not yet fully aware of the significance of women-related issues for the revitalization of Arab culture and traditions.

Men tend to forget that the issue of women's liberation and emancipation is closely linked to their own progress and development. And the question of national development is simply too important to leave to only one segment of the population, be it the male or the female one.

It is sad but true that the republican system failed to overcome the backward heritage of the Imamate regarding women's role in society. It is also true that some members of our society not only cling to and cherish backward views of women, but have even succeeded in influencing other parties to adopt some of their opinions. Not all aspects of our present state of under-development come from the far or near past. Putting the blame on the past is nothing but a desperate attempt to justify what we know is wrong and outdated behavior, but we persist in doing so in our social, political and cultural daily lives.

The Position of the Yemeni Women in Today's Society

There exists a deep rift between the female contribution to the national economy and the rights and position of women in society. Women constitute over 40% of the rural labor force[3], a figure that must have been much higher before the return of close to one million emigrants from Saudi Arabia in the wake of the Gulf War.

The force of repression on Yemeni women, resulting from ancient customs, can only be countered through an increased enrollment of the female part of society in the public domain, especially in the fields of education and health, but also technology.

The percentage of female enrollment in elementary secondary and higher education is still by far too low. Most disturbing is the high rate of illiteracy among the Yemeni women, reaching 93.5%[4]. This high figure is typically the result of early marriage, putting upon the shoulders of the young women not only the task of bearing and rearing children and taking care of the household, but also heavy tasks in agriculture and animal husbandry. Thus, the typical Yemeni girl invests most of her strength in daily chores and there remains no time to complete even the most basic level of formal education. Even among those women who have completed a certain level of training or higher education, the larger portion will inevitably limit their attention to the family and household, which is a loss for society as a whole.

In the more recently established sectors, women's share is only 22.6%[5]. These sectors are yet to implement new policies to benefit from women's capabilities in the areas of planning and production6. The total number of female students in graduate and undergraduate studies is very small.

In the field of education, the percentage of educated women contributing to the labor force in Yemen is only 5.6%[7]. The system of education and the fact that it is well developed only in the larger cities deprives women in the rural areas of educational opportunities. Since the Yemeni educational system takes a strictly theoretic approach, women do not get the opportunity to learn practical skills. Instead there are hundreds of female university graduates without work. Contrary to Saudi Arabia and other Gulf countries, the percentage of Yemeni women employed in banks and other commercial institutions is negligible. A higher level of economic prosperity would certainly encourage women to insist more forcefully upon obtaining their rights and freedom.

The laws concerning women in the constitution are not actually applied. The situation of women in Yemen can be compared to the situation of black people in the USA. The situation of Yemeni women is even worse due to the weakness of the judicial system and civil institutions and the strong power of conventions.

The 1977 constitution of the Yemen Arab Republic includes the following articles:

Article 34: "Women are the partners of men and they have the same rights and duties according to Islamic legislation and laws."

Article 35: "The government is responsible for supporting the family, maternity, senior citizens and handicapped people."

Article 43: "The basic rights are granted to all people on an equal basis regardless of religion, color, sex, language, origin or profession."

The 1972 constitution of the former People's Republic of Yemen is more specific about women's rights:

Article 27: "The government encourages marriage and the creation of families." The law also states that family relations are based upon equality between men and women."

Article 35: "People are equal in their rights and duties regardless of sex, social rules, religion, language, educational level or social rank."

Article 36: "The government guarantees equal rights for both men and women at all political, economic and social levels. The government shall also provide the necessary conditions enabling women to combine a social and public role with the role in their families. Women taking a public role are to be given special attention in terms of professional training. The government also provides kindergartens, parks and other facilities."

The family law in South Yemen before unification was in harmony with the above articles. However, the 1990 constitution of the Republic of Yemen (after unification) avoided even mentioning the word "woman". Instead, it only uses the phrase "citizen", implying both men and women.

Article 27 of the 1990 constitution says: "All citizens are equal before the law, they are equal in their rights and duties regardless of sex, color, origin, language, profession, social status or religion."

There exists a profound confusion between the text of the law and its interpretation. The Status Identification Law, for example, has been wrongly interpreted as giving the husband the right to divorce his wife if she leaves the house without his permission (e.g. going to the ballot box without his consent). In reality however, the law protects women, giving them the right to leave the house on their own on the grounds that there is a legal justification for such activities as going to work, helping disabled parents or taking part in elections.

The current labor laws are not applied equally towards women. Promotions, professional training and work opportunities, especially at high management levels, are mostly restricted to men. The same holds true for Labor Unions, where female workers are seldom represented, and so cannot exercise their rights. In other words, women have yet to raise their voices in labor unions and syndicates.

Without doubt, women themselves are partially responsible for their own oppression. Yemeni women may suffer a lot from injustice, but they will not make any effort to change their lives. Women do not fight for their rights and they do not involve themselves in organizations, associations or syndicates, thus they are unable to resist oppression by the male part of society.

Women coming from the countryside to larger cities suddenly find themselves confined to their homes. Conventions and customs do not encourage women in the cities to work.

In the cities, wealthy women have created their own tradition, despising public work. Staying idle at home and limiting their public appearance to the afternoon women's parties became a sign of virtue and social progress. Driving a car and wearing the veil are considered signs of high standing in the city[8]. Saudi women finally took to the streets in order to declare their right to drive a car. This happened in Riyadh on the eve of the Gulf War. In contrast, Yemeni women do not assert themselves by taking up their rightful position in the economic and social domains.

Women and the Parliamentary Elections of 1993

Democracy in Yemen came suddenly and quickly right after unification. Democracy and general elections are rightly perceived as the very conditions for unification to happen. Thus, unification and the establishment of democracy went hand in hand.

The question of women's role in the elections was heavily influenced by the politico-religious interpretation of the Islamists. Most other political parties did not agree with their interpretation, but they failed to take a clear stand and oppose this politicized Islamic interpretation put forth by the Islamists. On the contrary, some parties have even given in to this line of argumentation. They nominated very few women, arguing that women candidates would inevitably face much skepticism among the electorate because of the overall low level of political awareness.

The actual results, however, proved the opposite to be true. A good number of female nominees won second place in their constituencies. Samiah Al-Ahmadi, the PGC nominee in Rada', a city with a strong tribal character, received 1,200 votes. Samiah did not win, but she occupied the second place. Tayyibah Barakat, the YSP nominee in Hodeidah, received 2,286 votes. Radhyah Shamshir, YSP nominee in Sanaa, obtained 2,363 votes. Afrah ash-Shina, the PGC nominee in one of the constituencies in Aden, received 688 votes. Each one of these women occupied second place, just a few votes short of winning a seat in parliament[9].

The policy of the Islamist parties has been changing over the past few years. The policy propagated during the 1993 parliamentary elections is rather different from the one pronounced during the 1988 elections of the Shura Council in the former Yemen Arab Republic. At that time, the Islamists issued a fatwa (formal legal opinion by one or more Islamic religious leaders) declaring the nomination of women for general elections as "haram" - as incompatible with the rules of Islam. Initially women were seen unfit even to go to the ballot boxes. This attitude was dramatically reversed for the 1993 general elections when the same parties insisted upon the right of women to cast their own vote. However, this change of mind was carefully wrapped into another fatwa that stressed the religious obligation of women to submit to and follow their husbands.

A very similar development took place in Algeria, where the Islamic Salvation Front has declared by fatwa that the vote of a woman should be administered (and cast) by her husband. This is proof that the rights of a woman in wedlock are still at the mercy of her husband. Apparently it is easy for him to confiscate his wife's political and civil rights, especially when aided by religious legal decisions.

Islamist parties are keenly aware of the importance of women's votes. They made sure that women's votes were cast in due obedience to their husbands and for the best candidate (male, of course) from the viewpoint of the party to represent the interests of women in parliament.

The much cited argument by leading PGC politicians about "the low level of public awareness, making it difficult for women to enter parliament" has proved obsolete and outdated. Yet the same ideas keep on haunting the minds of the party leadership. The PGC's stand on women and elections was permeated by deep-running feelings of skepticism and confusion. As a result, the PGC nominated only two women candidates in the entire republic. The Yemen Socialist Party (YSP), which in the past used to be the kind of party that would guarantee a certain number of women to enter the People's Council in the South by simply putting them on one voting list, has also shied away from nominating many women candidates. Yet, the two women who actually made it into the parliament were both supported by the YSP.

Women's representation in judiciary institutions is either simply neglected or kept at a symbolic level at best. Women were represented by only one female member in the Supreme Election Committee[10]. It is quite obvious that the principle of equal rights among all members of society, as stated in the constitution and the laws, is still at the level of symbolic implementation. The role of women is being picked up by one or the other party for propaganda purposes, but usually neglected in the reality of political life.

It is a pity that some of the political parties which pride themselves in separating their political decisions from the fatwas of certain religious people ultimately fail to implement their own election programs. These parties, no matter how big and powerful, failed in recognizing the important role that women play in building modern nations. If they had only possessed the courage to stand up and openly back the role of women in the process of democratic elections, the advocates of political Islam would immediately have been placed in a defensive rather than an offensive position.

During the official election campaigns, Islamists have avoided openly rejecting the possibility of female parliamentarians; however, the argument that because she is a woman, a female cannot occupy any position which would put her in a position superior to that of a man, was frequently used in the unofficial election campaigns during the qat-chewing sessions.

The issue of women was down-played in the programs of most political parties. Women have been suffering the same kind of repression as the lower segments of our society. They have been despised in a manner similar to the way society despises certain classes, such as the Ahl al-Khums, the Dawashin and the Akhdam. These social distinctions still exist in our society. They have their roots in pre-Islamic times. Tendencies of social discrimination are deeply rooted in the minds of people in urban and rural areas alike. The Islah Party was the only party that pointed out this fact in its political program, but unfortunately it continued to practice against women the very discrimination it criticized.

Women's Issues in the Party Programs

The programs of the various political parties prior to the 1993 parliamentary elections took very different views on women's issues. They can be summarized as follows:

The People's General Congress
The PGC assures that women are partners of men and have a vital role to play in all fields of political and social life. Women have the same rights as men which are protected by Islam and the constitution. The PGC nominated two women, one in Aden and one in Rada'.

The Yemen Socialist Party
The YSP guarantees the right of women to equally participate in all political, economic, social and cultural aspects of life. Women should face no restrictions in participating in all fields of public life, freely working for the sake of public welfare.

The Islah Party

The Islah Party mentions an urgent need to give special attention to the education of girls. Women's rights are spelled out in the shari'ah, such as the right to education, work, property, inheritance, choice in marriage and participation in building the society. The party also stresses its resolution to resist any attempts aiming at the exploitation of women by misleading them or disrespecting their dignity.

The Haqq Party

The party calls for specifying fields of work suitable for women, such as education, health and family care. A framework of special laws should then be established for women that fits their nature and does not conflict with their other duties while preserving their rights. The party also calls for establishing schools and university branches for women only.

The Nasserite Popular Unification Organization

The party recognizes the role of women in society. Their rights should be well preserved according to the instructions of Islam and national heritage. Special care should be given to the family. All the rights of motherhood and childhood must be upheld.

The Nasserite Popular Correction Organization

The party encourages women to obtain their full rights in accordance with the Islamic shari'ah. All restrictions limiting the freedom of women in terms of their movements and participation in public life should be removed. This should be done in accordance with established social and religious values.

The Ba'th Party

The party did not specifically make mention of women's issues. It did, however, nominate two women. None of them were successful.

The complete absence, or should we say only weak presence, of women in the civil institutions of our society lies at the heart of the problem, thus, the opportunity for establishing a sound working relationship between men and women has been missed, and yet it is this relationship which is crucial for building a healthy, modern and democratic society.

The Yemeni Women's Union

The union is basically headed by women who are still clinging to old fashioned ideas that were common in the respective parts of Yemen before unification. In the southern part of the country the women's organization used to be part of the government. In the north six women's associations concerned with social work and charity were established in different cities. After unification, the executive office of the newly established Yemeni Women's Union came to consist of five members from the YSP, three from the PGC, one from the Islah Party and one from the independents. To the knowledge of this writer, the central committee has convened only once since the issuing of the governmental decree to merge the associations in the north and the union in the south. No unification conference was held.

The merger of the two parts of Yemen was accompanied by a lot of political maneuvering that strongly influenced most social organizations and unions. The Yemeni Women's Union was no exception. As a matter of fact, the political aspect has completely overtaken all the other noble goals and ideals. Decisive change or a loosening of the political grip cannot be expected for the near future. The membership is still the same as it was before unification. And it would be of little surprise, if the same faces come up again during the next elections.

The main challenge facing the Yemeni Women's Union (and indeed all public unions) is the question of how it can become an umbrella organization for all women irrespective of their political preferences or their social and cultural backgrounds. Can this development take place smoothly or will it be adversely affected by narrow political thinking? Can this fragile union possibly continue to exist while preserving the old leadership with its old methods?

These questions should concern all the women of our country. It is a sobering fact that most women's sectors were established by male politicians because of the inability of women to organize their own structures and activities.

Winning the right of nomination for women in the last parliamentary elections was a significant step forward. It affirms the right of women to participate in the affairs of the government and judiciary as well. It also made women's right for nomination an irrevocable fact, yet this right is still subject to the performance of the political parties that all too often act from political interest. It can be either encouraged or further impeded through fatwas issued by the religious leaders. The performance of the Yemeni Women's Union and other women's associations will influence the future political role of women. Developments regarding the political role of women is comparable to the development of democracy itself. The forces opposing democratic development will not back down easily but draw much strength from a long history of long-living traditions. The democratic forces, on the other hand, are not mature and strong enough to face these challenges with ease and confidence.

The liberation of women in Yemen has been facing and continues to face many obstacles and difficulties. It is a continuing battle to break the strength of age-old traditions, ultimately abolishing the logic of a men-only society. Cultural enlightenment will play a major role in this battle which has to be carried into all educational institutions and social organizations.

Conclusions

- Any further development in women-related issues is likely to take place primarily in the larger cities. Development should expand to cover the rural areas as well.
- Activities of the various women's associations and organizations mostly concentrates on social programs and charity. Women working in these associations are usually quite wealthy and form the upper level of society, yet women from all levels of society should participate in these activities.
- Women's participation in political life should be viewed as equally important as men's political participation. For women to participate fully, education is a key prerequisite; however the sad reality is that the percentage of illiterate women is still extremely high.
- Living conditions for women in the rural areas need serious change. Only after releasing rural women from their heavy daily chores can society prosper and the economy develop.
- Merely increasing the number of female university graduates will not automatically lead to improved conditions for the Yemeni society at large.
- The absence of women in the judiciary is a serious flaw in the development of a modern and democratic society.
- Education and cultural enlightenment should disseminate the basic values of modern life by challenging outmoded traditional values.
- The political parties issued only very general statements in addressing women's issues.
- Even though most political parties did exert much effort to gain women's votes, they failed to address the issue of women as a permanent and strategic issue.
- We have 350,000 out of nearly 500,000 registered female voters participated in the last elections; however, this figure does not correspond with the few female candidates who actually were nominated. One reason for this poor performance is the overall weakness of the women's participation in

parties, organizations and other institutions. Women's organizations are not taking the responsibility of defending their rights seriously enough.
- There is a lack of newspapers, magazines or other publications that deal with women's issues.
- There is a glaring absence of women in the political leadership of parties. No woman is present in the General Committee of the PGC, the Polit Bureau of the YSP or the High Preparatory Committee of the Islah Party. The same holds true for the rest of the parties, whether in government or in the opposition.

The current political trend of development, even if slowed down by traditionalists and conservatives, will benefit from initiatives that will open new horizons in support of women and consequently liberate society. It is important for women to participate in all fields of public life. Women are becoming increasingly qualified for leadership positions. The issue of political representation is always closely associated with political authority. When women share this authority along with men, political and social development will take place on a much higher level, but merely talking about a democratic society without balanced political representation of both men and women is bound to remain hypocritical.

---

1   "The Patriarchal Environment - A Research into Modern Arab Society by "Hisham Sharabi, Beirut 1987, p.64
2   ibid. p.66
3   "A Study on Democracy and the role of women in Rural Development" by Nabiha Abdulhamid, presented to the Regional Symposium for Women, Democracy and Modernization, UNESCO, Sanaa 14-18 April 1993, p.6
4   "The Reality of Women's Education in the Republic of Yemen" by Dr. Badr al-Aqbari, presented to the UNESCO Regional Symposium
5   "A Study on Democracy and the Role of Associations" by Shafiqa al-Juma'i, presented to the UNESCO Regional Symposium
6   "Yemeni Women between the Laws and the Reality of Implementation" by Fawziah Nu'man, presented to the UNESCO Regional Symposium, p.18
7   "The Reality of Women's Education....", p.15
8   The veil is a piece of cloth hiding the mouth and the nose; it may only disclose the eyes and for this reason reference to a woman's eyes is so important in Arab poetry.
9   "Report by the Technical Committee" of the Supreme Election Committee, May 1993, p.28,29
10 Mrs. Raqiyah Humaidan, a lawyer, was originally nominated by the YSP but finally entered the Supreme Election Committee as an independent member. The parliament, whose task it was to submit a list of possible candidates for the Supreme Election Committee to the Presidential Council, did not at first propose any women.

البون شاسعاً احياناً بين ماطرحتة الأحزاب في برامجها والسلوك الحقيقي لها في المعترك الفعلي للحياة السياسية وبالذات فيما يتعلق بالأيمان بمشاركة المرأة سياسياً.

أن النتائج التي افرزتها حرب السبعين يوماً (5مايو-7يوليو) ضد الأنفصاليين في سبيل ترسيخ الوحدة اليمنية لم تؤثر على المسار الديمقراطي للجمهورية اليمنية. وهذا ماتضمنه بيان مجلس الرئاسة الصادر في يوليو 1994م،والذي أكد على الثوابت الوطنية وفي مقدمتها اشاعة قيم الديمقراطية وحرية الرأي والرأي الأخر والتعددية السياسية والحزبية وهو الأمرالذي يعكس التوجه الصادق والأساس المتين الذي قامت عليه دولة الوحدة.

والأوراق التي يضمها هذا الكتاب هي تجميع لمختارات من البحوث والأوراق التي قدمت في عدة ندوات:-
الأولى نظمها فرع المؤتمر الشعبي العام بالتعاون مع اكاديمية الأساتذة من اجل السلام العالمي في صنعاء تحت عنوان (تطورات الديمقراطية في اليمن والعالم العربي) التي انعقدت في الفترة 22 23 يونيو 1989م.
والثانية ندوة نظمها فرع المؤتمر الشعبي العام بجامعة صنعاء(حول النظم الأنتخابية ومستقبل الديمقراطية في الجمهورية اليمنية) في الفترة 11-12 فبراير 1992م.
والثالثة ندوة حول (ضمانات لمستقبل الديمقراطية في اليمن) نظمها فرع المؤتمر الشعبي العام المنطقة الثانية بأمانة العاصمة في 17-18 مايو 1992م.

نأمل ان يكون هذا الأختيار للأوراق والبحوث التي يتضمنها هذا الكتاب مدخلاً متواضعاً لفهم ما يجري في اليمن ولاسيما الديمقراطية الوليدة فيها، وهي وان كانت جزءاً من (الموجة الثالثة) من الديمقراطية الا انها محكومة بشروطها الخاصة وبتاريخ قوي الحضور في مجتمع لا يتسم بالشفافية وبساطة التركيب، بل لعله احد المجتمعات العربية شديدة التعقيد على المستويات الأجتماعية والفكرية والسياسية، بسبب تعايش انماط عديدة من التركيبات الأجتماعية ومن الموروث التاريخي.

ولايفوتنا ان نشكر في الأخير المؤتمر الشعبي العام الذي قدم من خلال ندواتة المشار اليها مادة غنية اسهم تنوع الأفكار والمشاركين فيها في التعرف على الجوانب المختلفة للديمقراطية الوليدة في اليمن، ورؤية الأحزاب السياسية تجاهها. كما نتوجه بالشكر الى اكاديمية الأساتذة من اجل السلام العالمي التي شاركت في تنظيم الندوة الأولى ومولت طباعة هذا الكتاب.وكان للدكتور محمد شرف الدين فضل القيام بترجمة الغالب من هذه المواد الى اللغة الأنجليزية.

هذا والله من وراء القصد
أمة العليم السوسوه
صنعاء سبتمبر 1994 م

ويبدو ان العملية بأسرها تتعلق بالجانب الأقتصادي اذ سيترتب على حلها ولو جزئياً او على بقائها دون حل مصير الديمقراطية والتعددية.

اما ورقة الدكتور **منصور عزيز الزنداني** فقد تركزت حول سياسات الدول الكبرى تجاه ديمقراطيات العالم الثالث فبرغم شعور دول الجنوب بالسعادة لبروز الديمقراطية واعتبارها غاية ووسيلة لتحقيق ماتطمح اليه، وللتخلص من الفساد السياسي الذي تجرعته، الا ان هذه الامال تظل محفوفة بالمخاطر الداخلية والخارجية. ويبدي قلقه من موضوع نقل واختيار الأنموذج الديمقراطي المعين الذي لابد من تلازمه مع نقل القيم الغربية الى الدول المستقبلة لهذه النماذج، ويؤكد على مسألة ذوبان الشخصية الوطنية في تبعيته للأ نموذج.

أما ضمانات الديمقراطية في اليمن كما يراها الدكتور **محمد أحمد السعيدي** فانها متعددة،واساسها الأستقرار الأقتصادي والأمني بالأضافة الى المزيد من المشاركة في صنع القرارت المصيرية وحرية التعبير، ويدافع الدكتور السعيدي عن فكرة وجود بذور الفكر الديمقراطي في اساس القبيلة ونظام حياتها، ولايوافق على ان الغرب هو زارع الفكرة بالذات في الدول التي استعمرها. ويشير الى عدد من العوامل الأضافية التي تؤدي الى رسوخ النظام الديمقراطي والعيش به وعلى رأس ذلك النظام التشريعي والدستوري والقانوني السليم.
اما هيئات المجتمع المدني ومشاركتها الفاعلة المستقلة بالأضافة الى دعم مجالس الحكم المحلي تمثل اضافة حقيقية الى ضمانات استمرار الحياه الديمقراطية في اليمن.

وجاءت ورقة **فريتز بيبنبرج** الألماني لتعرض بصورة سريعة البدايات التي حاولت السير نحو الديمقراطية في اليمن شمالا وجنوباً. ويبدو منها ان البدايات في الجنوب كانت متأثرة بنمط جاهز هو النمط الغربي بحكم وجود المستعمر. ويشير مستنداً الى كتاب الدكتور قائد طربوش الى ما حدث في لحج وعدن وأبين. وفي مقدمة استعراضه للأنتخابات يحدثنا عن ديمقراطية دينية هي الشورى. ويذكر ان هناك من يعادل بين هذا المفهوم والديمقراطية دون ان يطرح رايه بل لعله يبدو قريباً من هذا الرأي عندما يعلن ان الديمقراطية البرلمانية رغم تقدمها ليست بأي حال من الأحوال صورة الديمقراطية الوحيدة.
ولاشك في أن جهده في رصد الأحداث او الوسائل الأيضاحية التي اوردها تعطي القاري خريطة واضحة لما تم يوم ٢٧ ابريل ١٩٩٣م مبيناً ذلك من خلال وثائق اللجنة الفنية للجنة العليا للأنتخابات الصورة الكاملة.

اما ورقة **أمة العليم السوسوه** حول المرأة والديمقراطية فقد حاولت تبيان جزيء من جزيئات الحياة في اليمن، وهي مهمة لكشف الفرق بين الأطروحات النظرية وخلفيات المجتمع الثقافية والسياسية التي تتحكم في نتائج حياتنا وافعالنا، حيث كان

والنقد الذي يوجهه الدكتور محمد جعفر قاسم الى قانون الأنتخابات في اليمن ينطلق من حرصه على تأسيس نظام قادر على التطور حتى تبدأ تجربة الديمقراطية في اليمن من اساس سليم. ومن الواضح انه يعرض خبرة ودراسة طويلة لأشكال قوانين الانتخابات في عدة بلدان اوربية بالدرجة الاولى دون ان يعني ذلك،انه لم ياخذ تجارب الاقطار العربية والافريقية والاسيوية بالاعتبار وهو يفكر باليمن. وهناك الكثير مما يجب على الديمقراطية الوليدة في اليمن ان تتعلمه من تجارب الشعوب الاخرى التي سبقتها الى انواع الحكم الديمقراطي.

والورقة تناقش التفاصيل القانونية التي تترتب عليها اجراءات عملية تؤثر في سير الانتخابات ونتائجها كما تلقي ضوءًا على المزايا والثغرات القائمة في قانون الانتخابات النافذ، بينما تهتم ورقة الدكتور احمد عبد الرحمن شرف الدين بالأسس والمبادىء التي يقوم عليها حق الانتخابات، مثل المساواة والشخصية، اي ممارسة الحق بالأصالة لا بالأنابة. وهذه مشكلة واجهتها الجزائر حيث سمح للزوج بالتصويت بالأنابة عن زوجته وفي هذا الغاء لمبداء الشخصية. وينبه صاحب الورقة الى ضرورة حل مشكلة اصوات المهاجرين والمنقولين من اماكن عملهم داخل اليمن مادام توفرالشرطان الاساسيان وهما:-الجنسية اليمنية وبلوغ الثامنة عشرة من العمر.

ورغم غلبة الجانب الوصفي على ورقة الهام محمد مانع عن الجزائر لكنها تقدم نموذجًا عن قطر عربي، وترينا ان اي تجاوز للأسس الدستورية في قانون الأنتخابات تترتب عليه مشكلات سياسية ذات اثر بالغ الخطورة في تطور الحياة الديمقراطية والأجتماعية، وتهدد في الاساس كل البنيان الذي يقوم عليه الأستقرار وامكان التداول السلمي للسلطة.

وتطرح ورقة أحمد علي الوادعي اسئلة اساسية ومطلقة وفي نفس الوقت تعتبر الوحيدة التي تعلن ان الأختيار في اليمن قبل الوحدة وبعده قد سار على النمط الليبرالي الغربي الذي انتجتة الرأسمالية وهي مع الديمقراطية موطن هذين النظامين. وهوما لاتعمله الاوراق الاخرى او ما تحاول ان تهمله لصالح حديث عن ديمقراطية غامضة.

وتخوف صاحب الورقة من النتائج التي يمكن ان تصل اليها اليمن بسب ضعف عدد من الأسس اللازمة لنمو ديمقراطية قادرة على الأستمرار والبقاء، بينما تتميز الوحدة بأنها أوفر حظًا في وعي الناس. اما ان تكون النتيجة بقاء البلاد متمتعة بالوحدة ولكن بلا ديمقراطية فذلك دون شك سيكون حصيلة نجاح او فشل القوى التي تدافع عن الديمقراطية، وذلك يتطلب في فرصة اخرى دراسة الأساس الأجتماعي للديمقراطية في اليمن، وهل يمكن لهذه القوى ان تجعل من الديمقراطية التي فاجأت الجميع قابلة للنمو والرسوخ ؟ وهل يمكن ان يلغي اليمنيون وهم يمارسون الديمقراطية تلك الحقيقة الماثلة في ان حزبين شموليين سابقين هما في مقدمة الذين يتحمسون للديمقراطية؟

ورقة <u>أحمد محمد الحربي</u> تقدم في هذا السياق نبذة تاريخية عن أشكال التعاون وتطورها لاسيما في القرية اليمنية التي عرفت منذ قرون هذا النوع من التضامن الأجتماعي، الذي نشأ داخل علاقات العمل في الزراعة والري وهو يوضح في نفس الوقت لا العلاقات التعاونية فحسب بل ايضاً صورتوزيع السلطات في القرية اليمنية وطرق حل النزاع الذي ينشأ في خضم العمل والتعاون.

وقد شهدت هذه الأشكال من نظم العمل والتعاون وطرق حل النزاع تطوراً طويلاً يعادل تاريخ نشأتها وتطورها منذ عهد ماقبل الأسلام الى هذه الأيام. وان كان من الصعب الجزم بتاريخ محدد لنشأتها رغم انها رافقت ظهور التجمعات السكنية المستقرة في الريف وفي الدولة-المدينة.

ان تطور العمل التعاوني في السنوات الاخيرة قد أحدث حركة اجتماعية سياسية وأصبحت هذه الحركة تساهم في تقديم الخدمات الى جمهور غفير في الريف الذي يشكل ساكنوه نحو ٨٨٪ من السكان.

ان ظهور حركة التعاون في حد ذاته دليل على عدم قدرة الحكومة المركزية القيام باعباء الخدمات الأجتماعية بشكل مرض. ولاشك ان مصير هذه الحركة يتوقف، من حيث الفاعلية والتطور، ومن حيث القدرة، على جعلها جزءاً مؤثراً من النظام اللامركزي الذي وعدت به كل الأحزاب الكبيرة والصغيرة في برامجها الأنتخابية.

وأحمد الحربي عضو عامل نشيط في تلك الحركة، ومن هنا فان ورقتة تقدم الى جانب الوصف التاريخي والاجتماعي العام خبرة شخصية في هذا المجال. ومن السهولة التطور في مفهوم المشاركة السياسية التي عاشتها خلفيات سياسية متعددة في ظل الأجماع على الميثاق الوطني الذي اقر باستفتاء شعبي في عام ١٩٨١م.

ورقة الدكتور <u>سعد الدين ابراهيم</u> تستعرض رياح الديمقراطية التي هبت على اقطار الوطن العربي، وفي هذا السياق يبدو ان عرب اليمن يشكلون رافداً اساسياً في هذا الأطار العربي الكبير، وفي الجزء الذي شهد قيام الأسلام، ويعتبر اليوم اغنى اقليم عربي بالثروة النفطية، التي يدمج اقتصادها بحركة المراكز الاوربية والامريكية.

وجاءت الاوراق الثلاث التالية التي قدمت في ندوة عن النظام الأنتخابي ومستقبل الديمقراطية في اليمن متكاملة بعض الشىء، فقد اهتم الدكتور <u>أحمد عبد الرحمن شرف الدين</u> بالحديث عن المبادى الأساسية لقوانين الأنتخابات لما لها من دور مؤثر في انتاج اي ديمقراطية سليمة تملك اساساً للتطور.

ونشأة الديمقراطية في اقطار الوطن العربي تشهد صراعات على هذه القوانين، ومثال الجزائر اشهر من يعرف في هذا الشان.

ورقة <u>الهام محمد مانع</u> تبسط الظروف التي احاطت بقانون الأنتخابات في الجزائر والصعوبات التي اكتنفت تلك التجربة، وهي تصف لا تطور النزاع على قانون الأنتخابات وتجربة الأقتراع الديمقراطي التي شهدتها الجزائر بعد حكم شمولي طويل فحسب، بل والظروف العينية التي حكمت التجربة وادت الى النتيجة المعروفة.

بســـم الله الرحمن الرحيم

مـقدمة

أختيرت الاوراق التي يضمها هذا الكتاب لكي تعطي معاً صورة عن الديموقراطيـــة في اليمن وتطبيقها العملي وبعض ملامحها التي يمكن ان تساعد في تدريب المواطنــين على حكم أنفسهم بأنفسهم.

ورقة محمد شاهر حسن: وقد ركزت على تبيان تطور المسار الديمقراطي عندمـا عرضت الأفكار والأسس السياسية التي حكمت نشأت وتطور المؤتمر الشعبي العام باعتباره حزباً كبيراً أصبح بعد الوحدة أحد الأحزاب التي شــكلت تجربــة التعدديــة السياسية التي دخلت نطاق التجربة في أنتخابات ٢٧ ابريل ١٩٩٣م .

وتناولت التفصيلات علاقة الحقائق والوقائع التي ذكرها بآفاق التطور الديمقراطي في اليمن. ولاشك في أن الديمقراطية الراسخة هي تلك التي تنشأ في القاعدة وتكون كمـا يقول (دي توكفيل):-" شكل حكم الذات "، اي قـدرة التعاونيـات، والمـدارس، والمعـاهد العلمية، وكل منظمات المجتمع المدني، على حكم نفسها دون حاجـة الى رقابــة أو توجيه. ويمكن أن تكون التعاونيـات بعد الغاء نظام الحزب الواحد اساسـاً وطيداً للمجتمع المدني ومدرسة للديمقراطية الفاعلة.

كما ان استقلال النقابات والمنظمات الأجتماعية عن الأحزاب والدولة معاً سوف يجعل هذا الأساس ضماناً لتفاعل المجتمع المدنــي والسياسي، وهو الأساس الحقيقي لكل ديمقراطية يكتب لها الأستمرار.

ورقة الدكتور أحمد محمد الكبسي أختيرت لأنها تقدم عرضاً تاريخياً موجزاً لتطور مفهوم الديمقراطية منذ حركة عام ١٩٤٨م وميثاقها الوطني المقدس حتى هذه الأيام، وهي تقتصر على تطور المفهوم الديمقراطي فيما كان يعرف بشمال اليمن قبـل الوحدة. وبحكم تخصص صاحبها وعمله في الجامعة فأنه يتتبع تاريخ النشأة محـاولاً الأمساك بخيط تطورها. وبين الدكتور الكبسي في بحثه الأساس الدستوري والقـانوني للعمل الديمقراطي حتى الحوار الوطني وأقرار الميثاق الوطني للمؤتمر الشعبي العام.

التطورات الديمقراطية في الجمهورية اليمنية

أمة العليم السوسوه

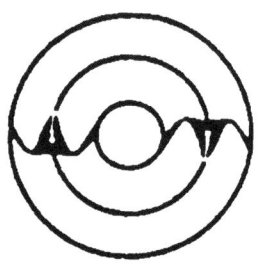

أكاديمية الأساتذة من أجل السلام العالمي

Bei Fragen zur Produktsicherheit wenden Sie sich bitte an:
If you have any questions regarding product safety,
please contact:

Walter de Gruyter GmbH
Genthiner Straße 13
10785 Berlin
productsafety@degruyterbrill.com